LEADING WORKSHOPS, SEMINARS, AND TRAINING SESSIONS

LEADING WORKSHOPS, SEMINARS, AND TRAINING SESSIONS

Great ideas, information, and inspiration

Helen Angus

Self-Counsel Press
(*a division of*)
International Self-Counsel Press Ltd.

First edition: April, 1993

Canadian Cataloguing in Publication Data
   Angus, Helen Y.
   Leading workshops, seminars, and training sessions
   (Self-counsel business series)
   ISBN 0-88908-279-0
   1. Workshops (Adult education) — Handbooks, manuals, etc.
2. Seminars — Handbooks, manuals, etc. I. Title. II. Series.
LC44.A53 1993   374'.1122   C93-091183-0

Cover photography by Terry Guscott, ATN Visuals, Vancouver, B.C.

Self-Counsel Press
(*a division of*)
International Self-Counsel Press Ltd.

1481 Charlotte Road
North Vancouver, British Columbia
V7J 1H1

1704 N. State Street
Bellingham, Washington
98225

CONTENTS

Talk one to one.

APPENDIXES

CHECKLISTS

FIGURES

SAMPLES

Preface

This book is written for anyone who is called upon to make presentations, lead meetings, or conduct training sessions. It is specially designed as a practical guide, with a minimum of theory. It gives tried and tested tips and techniques for imparting work-related knowledge, information, and skills to others, whether in a classroom, workshop, small meeting, or large group at a conference. It is for use both by the novice and the more experienced alike, so that all will be able to develop and improve their skills, become more comfortable in the leading role, and derive satisfaction from even more successful presentations.

Perhaps you have never given a talk or lead a workshop before, or you are called upon to do it infrequently. Or, perhaps you make presentations regularly — even by choice!

This type of public session is not the same as making a speech to persuade and convince, or just to give straight information — what we normally think of as "public speaking." Making presentations, leading workshops, and running training sessions differ because they have to ensure some specific learning takes place. For example, if you are a technical writer, you will call upon different skills to run a training workshop for your peers than you would to make a short speech to strangers explaining what you do for a living. In the latter case, you have to be able to impart your knowledge succinctly and in an interesting manner. But in the former case, you have to understand how to work with a group, how people learn, and how to draw them into your own experience so they go away with increased, practical knowledge.

In a work setting, those who are seen as "experts," whether it is because of their experience or particular knowledge and skills, may be asked to pass on their expertise to other employees in meetings or in workshops. There may be times when new or different products, services, systems, procedures, or legal requirements have to be explained to the staff. In small businesses, because of limited resources, internal "experts" often have to undertake this instructional and training role. Doing so effectively requires an additional set of skills that may not yet be fully developed.

Consultants and salespeople are continually instructing customers and clients in the use of their products or services. Professionals, such as teachers, lawyers, or engineers, may be asked to give special presentations or speak to meetings of their colleagues or professional association or give seminars at conferences.

Specialists who establish themselves as consultants may offer training sessions in client organizations, passing on their knowledge and skills, conducting public seminars and workshops, and/or speaking at conferences. There is an increased call for full-time and part-time trainers and instructors in their areas of professional competence, often working through training organizations and business and educational institutions.

Anyone in these situations will benefit from adding to their existing proficiencies the special skills needed to communicate effectively with others in a workshop, seminar, or training session.

1 *What have I got myself into?*

So you have been asked to run a seminar, lead a workshop, or develop a training session. Where do you begin? Perhaps you are very motivated, keen, and confident. More likely, though, you also feel some apprehension, especially if this is a situation you have not dealt with before.

a. I THINK I CAN, I THINK I CAN...

Building your own self-confidence is the first step to success, because if you are confident, your audience will feel positive and enthusiastic. Your confidence will communicate itself to your audience. But being self-confident about doing something new in front of many people isn't an easy thing to achieve.

A while ago, I spoke with an insurance and investment specialist who is often asked to speak to groups about good sales techniques. Peter is very successful in his job and comfortable talking one on one, but the idea of standing up and talking in front of a group really scared him. He finally decided that he had to accept the challenge. He had recently read about the use of "positive visualization" and we discussed how he could apply some of these strategies to his own situation.

Often, people making presentations turn themselves off by imagining the worst; they focus on all the dreadful things that could go wrong. But by using those same visualization techniques, you can instead emphasize the positives of the situation. For example, you might think about your years of experience and visualize yourself successfully making your presentation in front of a group. Many top athletes use this technique before a competition. They visualize themselves crossing the finish line and they actually "hear" the crowd cheering as they are presented with the gold medal.

Peter used this technique to prepare for a presentation. He also took the time to list all the positives he has going for him:

(a) The audience really wants to hear from him and feels very favorable about him.

(b) He is very knowledgeable and successful in his profession, so he already has high credibility.

(c) He is keen to share his knowledge and the benefits of his considerable experience with others.

(d) He presents himself well; he normally speaks clearly and is easy to understand. He is pleasant, has an agreeable appearance, and no distracting mannerisms.

(e) He is smart enough to do the necessary preparation and organize his ideas to suit the group.

When we met again recently, Peter was pleased to tell me the good news: he had actually "forced" himself to speak at a conference and had an excellent reception. He is still anxious, but now knows he can do it. With practice, he will gain confidence and will probably manage to improve his style. Peter will be more willing to accept future invitations and he might even start to seek out opportunities to speak.

...think positive! No doubt you also ...lot going for you, just like Peter, and ...ust need to add to your professional ...wledge and skills by practicing and im...oving your presentation skills. So let us ...art right now. Begin to build your self-confidence by learning more about your audience.

b. YOUR AUDIENCE — WHAT MAKES THEM TICK?

When you are planning a presentation for adults, you need to consider the characteristics of your audience. Adults bring to a learning arena very different experience than children or students in a traditional school setting. Understanding these characteristics is vital to effectively communicating with your audience.

This is not a text book, and you don't need to study the jargon of professional adult educators. However, you can benefit from reviewing these key points that have proven helpful for other leaders and trainers.

1. Experience

Adults have existing experience, knowledge, and skills that affect their ability to learn. If you recognize and point out your participants' experience and skills, you will enhance their self-esteem and motivation. Find out what participants already know; this is the base on which to build their new skills.

2. Self-concept

Adults may have either a positive or negative perception of themselves, known as self-concept. Or they may have a fairly healthy self-concept about their ability to do a job, but have misgivings about learning new things. Often negative self-concept is the result of poor previous experiences in an education or training setting.

Self-concept can also be based on a person's beliefs about the effects of aging on their ability to learn. Or perhaps people feel that they are "out of practice" for learning something new.

Going into a presentation, you may not know how everyone in your audience feels about learning and about being in that particular situation. You may have to spend some time finding out by asking questions and trying to draw out their feelings. You should be prepared to spend some time building self-esteem. As you go along you can get rid of potential barriers by reviewing what has been accomplished, what skills participants have gained, and how this new knowledge will benefit them after the seminar or workshop is completed.

3. Expectations

Adults expect professionalism from trainers and instructors. They assume that the leader is knowledgeable and skilled and has the ability to pass those skills on. Adults expect to be treated courteously and with dignity and respect as individuals and as a group. They do not want to waste time and expect it to be used profitably. If they (or their employers) are paying for the experience, they expect value for money.

4. Anxiety

In a learning situation, adults are often anxious about the possibility of personal or professional failure or appearing foolish. These emotions, which can create barriers to the learning process, often stem from deeper feelings of inadequacy. Perhaps Joe is concerned that new techniques will be too difficult to learn because he always had trouble in school. Or Joan worries that the new computer system she is to be trained on is a threat to the security of her job and her place as "the computer expert" based on her knowledge and years of experience. For some, the perception of the change from "manager" to "learner" can be threatening because they feel they aren't in control.

Generally, adults may feel tense at the prospect of change and of encountering the unknown.

c. HELPING YOUR AUDIENCE LEARN

You've probably attended a seminar where the speaker put the audience to sleep. And you've also probably attended a workshop or speech where you have left motivated, inspired, and excited to try out your newly learned skills or pass on your just-acquired information. What is the difference between the two? What helps an audience tune into the speaker and his or her words and methods?

The answer to that comes just as much from the audience as from the speaker. You, as leader of a seminar, must understand what makes an audience *want* to learn and to listen.

1. Interest and motivation

You can't go into a seminar with a dictatorial attitude that you will teach and your audience will learn — or else! Usually, adults will only learn what they want to learn. They are also more motivated to learn when they can see the usefulness and relevance of the particular information or skills. Adult learning often centers on answering needs or solving problems, and the problems must be realistic.

For example, if you are going to run a training session in the local library on the new copyright regulations, it isn't enough to recite the law. You need to give realistic examples of how this affects the library and its patrons with its photocopying policy, how they might budget for buying extra copies of books, why the copyright owner has a right to be protected, etc. Keep your audience motivated by applying examples directly to their specific situation.

2. Readiness

Success or failure is greatly determined by the learner already having the background skills or knowledge essential for acquiring the new skills or knowledge. The instruction must be given at an appropriate time: when there is a need for it and when it can be applied as soon as possible afterwards.

3. Organization

Learning is easier and more rapid when the information (or the content) is structured in a logical and progressive way. As well, the organization of the process itself can enhance learning. That is, you may be training employees in a ten-step safety program, so naturally your presentation would be structured to introduce, in order, steps one through ten. But within that structure, you might organize the process of teaching each step by first explaining, then demonstrating, and finally, allowing participants to practice.

It is also helpful to explain the organizational structure of the presentation right at the start. Tell your audience what your goals are, how you will approach the topic, and what they can expect throughout the session. This makes everyone feel more comfortable and allows your audience to better organize their own learning.

4. Open communication

Adults learn best through two-way communication where there are opportunities for questions, comments, airing of concerns, and feedback. Group members can contribute to the learning process and learn from each other, especially since they often have background knowledge to benefit everyone. Open communication also creates a less threatening atmosphere.

5. Participation

Adults learn best by doing: they learn more and remember it better and for longer. You will find that it's easier to gain and maintain interest and motivation through active involvement. As well, an informal atmosphere is also usually more effective than a highly structured, formal setting.

6. Positive, reinforcing environment

If you encourage your audience for what is achieved, rather than comment on errors, lack of progress, etc., you are more likely to increase motivation. When you encourage the participants you help break down the barriers that are raised by negative feelings, such as anxiety, frustration, and boredom. When individuals feel respected and well treated, their performance improves.

7. Immediate feedback

Everyone responds well to recognition of achievement. Adults prefer to know immediately about their progress so that if they need to improve, they can take the necessary corrective action. Constructive criticism is obviously the preferred method since adults want guidance rather than grades.

8. Variety

Adults like variety. Use whatever devices are available to you to increase interest levels. You can present the same information by lecture, handout, overhead projector, slide show, videotape, role playing, or a combination of these and other techniques.

You need to use repetition to help your audience understand your content and absorb new information. But repetition can also be boring. Use various presentation techniques such as those mentioned above to repeat your ideas and keep your audience interested.

d. DIFFERENT PEOPLE, DIFFERENT STYLES

Everyone has a different way of receiving, processing, and applying information. As an instructor, you should be prepared to accommodate these differences.

Most of us tend to pass on information in the way we personally prefer to receive it — in other words, we teach as we would like to learn. But your way might not be the best way to communicate to someone else.

For example, you might find the most efficient way to learn a new computer program is by using the on-line tutorial and practicing with the files on the training disk. If you tell your staff that they must also learn the program by using the same tutorial, you might have some frustrated learners. Another computer user might learn more effectively by having someone sit down and do a hands-on demonstration. Yet another might prefer to read the program manual and then apply what he or she has learned directly to a work-related project.

There has been a good deal of research in the area of different learning styles. The basic concepts are described below.

1. Processing information

We process information and learn through our senses. Researchers have shown that we all use all of our senses, but tend to use one predominantly. Thus, most of us are either *visuals*, *auditories*, or *kinaesthetics*.

(a) Visuals

Visuals depend more on their sight than on their hearing or touch to make sense of what they perceive. They often use, and respond well to, words and phrases that evoke visual images. They like to see things happen and can take in a great deal by watching and observing.

Visuals benefit from slide presentations, overhead transparencies, board work, graphs, and diagrams. Videotapes, films, and handouts are also very helpful.

Color can be used to good effect with visuals, especially if you make up a color-code system. For example, you could print or underline all your headings and main points in one color and your subheads in another color. This makes the points stand out and helps many people remember better. It also adds variety.

I often print handouts on different colored paper organized by topics. This makes it easier for participants to refer to material throughout and after my presentation. For example, if I have handed out 10 different exercises, it is generally easier for people to find the correct page if I say, "Now, if you will turn to the blue page in your package...."

(b) Auditories

Auditories take in and remember through sounds, using their ears and their voices. They often repeat words to learn them and respond well to patterns of sound, rhythm, music, and song. They like to talk through problems and often use phrases like "Sounds right to me," and "I hear what you are saying." Their speech is characterized by vocal variety.

When you use visual aids in your presentation, you will help the auditories in your audience by explaining out loud the points you are trying to make in the graphics, slide show, etc.

(c) Kinaesthetics

Kinaesthetics like to touch, move, be physically involved, and be as active as possible. They like to act out, produce, make a project, experiment, and practice.

If you use a variety of presentation methods, you are likely to accommodate the learning needs of all three types. At the same time, you will provide variety in your presentation, which will please everyone and heighten interest and motivation.

2. Listening and thinking

There has been a lot of talk in recent years about people using different parts of their brains for various tasks. Perhaps you have been described as "left brained" if you are very logical and orderly. Or, if you are creative and spontaneous, you may have been labelled as "right brained."

Research does show that the way individuals view the world, how they listen and think, and how they make decisions is affected by which part of the brain is dominant. There are four main types of listeners:

(a) *Movers* are the quick thinkers in your audience. They are action-oriented, "take-charge" types. Their focus is on speed and action. They listen best to a presentation that is a brief, logical summary with recommended action.

(b) *Arrangers* like and need details and summaries. They prefer that time and attention be given to each detail; they may seem like plodders. They listen best to a presentation that is detailed, accurate, thorough, logical, and sequential.

Arrangers actually read any supplementary material that is given out. They may be hard to convince, but once convinced, they stay loyal and firm. Arrangers are often found in professions such as accounting, engineering, and computer science.

(c) *Visionaries* tend toward a global view and may be seen as dreamers. They like pictures and color. They listen best to information in which the goals and purpose are given first; then they will accept the elements that go into the desired results.

(d) *Relaters* value people and relationships and respond well to words and phrases evoking feelings. They listen best to information that is presented in terms of its impact on people. They want to know how people will feel. Relaters are often found in the helping professions: teaching, nursing, and social work, for example.

If you can, determine which type of listeners and thinkers will be in your audience when you plan your presentation. Of course, this is not always possible and most groups have a mixture of types. But sometimes, particularly if you are making a presentation to a group of people all from one occupation, you can use the theories of "types" of learners to your advantage.

Whatever style you choose, DO NOT make the entire presentation in a style that matches only your own listening and thinking style. Most audience members will have elements of all four styles in their personal learning and thinking style.

e. YOU CAN'T TEACH AN OLD DOG NEW TRICKS — OR CAN YOU?

Many people believe "you can't teach an old dog new tricks." They may also believe that they themselves are "old dogs" — even if they're only 30! "Learning is for kids" is their attitude, so they *won't* learn because they're convinced they *can't* learn.

The truth is, older people may learn *better* than younger people for the following reasons:

(a) They are often more motivated to learn, especially if they can see the relevance to their lives.

(b) Their maturity can help them apply themselves so they can achieve valued outcomes.

(c) They often already have a body of related experience, knowledge, and skills on which to build.

(d) They may have developed effective learning skills over time.

No matter what your age, keeping the mind fit is like keeping the body fit. You have to eat well (good nutrition helps the memory) and stay in shape. You, as seminar leader, can help learners do this by showing them how to flex their brain power. The brain is wonderfully adaptable and capable of handling new things.

However, the brain does change and function differently as we age. Here are some general observations about the aging brain:

(a) Perceptual speed or the ability to grasp new information increases.

(b) Memory span is likely to remain stable.

(c) Reaction time declines, so, for instance, older drivers might react less quickly to sudden occurrences.

(d) Older people require more information than younger people to attain confidence in their judgments.

(e) Older people are better at using what they learn than they are at explaining it.

(f) Older people have a harder time modifying wrong impressions once they are formed; a correct first impression is vital.

Remember that these are generalizations.

The older the person, the more entrenched his or her own style of learning usually is. Adult learners may be frustrated if you try to instruct by using only one style — the style in which you personally learn best. You want to encourage adults to learn in their own style, but introduce them to other styles if those are more appropriate.

f. THANKS FOR THE MEMORIES...

There is no learning unless you remember what you learn, and many adult learners are concerned that they will not retain what they have taken in. Memory and the process of remembering can be thought of as a three-R process where the learner must —

(a) *register* the information,

(b) *retain* or "file" the information, and

(c) *recall* or *retrieve* the information later.

When a person has difficulty remembering, it is usually only part of the process that is at fault rather than the whole memory system.

1. Registering

You need to help learners register the information in the first place. If you can inspire a positive attitude and focus people's interest and attention, you will motivate people to want to remember.

Short-term memory retention is easily disturbed by aging and this decline is evident even from the early twenties. It is even worse if some conflicting activity intervenes and interferes during the registering period, when new information is being taken in.

2. Retaining

Retaining is the process of storing the information once it has been registered. You must organize and present material so that it will register in a meaningful way and be easier to retain. New information must relate to what is already known; it helps if it is organized so that the learner can easily classify it and put it in the proper order. We place and store information in our long-term memory using imagery, association, and organization.

Learners may have some difficulty escaping from immediate associations, excluding unwanted material, and selecting relevant material. They need to work at overcoming previous associations and developing new ones. An individual may have performed a work-related activity the same way for many years, but now may have to do it differently. First, the worker must feel the new way is better, then work hard to learn the new method. The previous method is automatic and will have to be "unlearned" before new learning can be effective. The same holds true for changing ways of thinking.

Adults can improve their short-term memory retention and recall by using self-reminding devices such as mnemonics (memory "tricks"), lists, etc. Encourage adult learners to come up with their own memory devices or give them some of your own. Often the less sensible (or the sillier) the better, since these are the ones that really stick in the brain! I was taught "Sam's Horse Must Eat Oats" for remembering the names of the Great Lakes. The first letter of each word in the phrase represents the first letter of each of the lakes from east to west: Superior, Huron, Michigan, Erie, Ontario.

3. Retrieving

Retrieval is the process of finding the information in your memory after it has been registered and retained. You also have to recognize the correct information when you recall it. You must help learners register and retain what they learn and then have them practice retrieving it.

Registering, retaining, and retrieving information isn't as easy as it looks. For instance, recipients of purely "passive learning" (e.g., reading, or listening only), forget 50% of the material within 48 hours, and a further 25% within two weeks!

Real involvement is needed: activities that involve thinking, discussion, problem-solving, practicing, or anything else that allows the participants to use the material in a meaningful way. This kind of involving activity is needed both while learning and as soon as possible afterwards in order to cement it into the memory. Practice is effective for the young, but much more so for adults.

g. THOSE WHO CAN ... TEACH!

The saying, "Those who can, do. Those who can't, teach." distinguishes between those who *do* and those who *teach* and implies that people rarely are good at both. As a seminar leader, you will put the lie to this. You must first be a "doer" with the necessary level of skills and knowledge to pass on to others. However, it is your ability to teach, to help others gain your knowledge, that is probably even more important because, without it, the material will not be passed on at all!

In his book, *Cornerstones of a Motivating Instructor*, Stanley Wlodowski outlines the predominant features a successful teacher strives for:

(a) *Expertise:* Knows something beneficial to adults and knows the subject well. Is prepared to convey knowledge.

(b) *Empathy:* Has a realistic understanding of students' needs and expectations. Adapts instruction to students' level of expertise and skill. Continually considers the students' perspective.

(c) *Enthusiasm:* Cares about and values what is being taught. Expresses commitment to the topic with appropriate degrees of emotion, animation, and energy.

(d) *Clarity:* Provides additional/alternative instruction if the initial presentation is unclear. Instruction is understood and followed by most students.

By keeping these ideals in mind when planning and conducting your seminar, you will help your students become "doers," too!

2 *Preparing a winning presentation*

In this chapter, we look at how to prepare for different types of presentations, whether they are for a small or large group, for instruction or training in specific skills, processes or procedures, or for passing on information or knowledge to be applied in a work situation. Straightforward presentations are also be considered, as are talks where there is less emphasis on the instructing/learning aspect.

a. CONDUCT A NEEDS ANALYSIS

Suppose you have to develop an instructional session to suit particular job-related needs. For example, perhaps it is your job to train the data entry department in a new method of reporting and recording sales information. In order to find out what the specific needs are of the people you will be training, you need to conduct a *needs analysis*. You can do this yourself directly or have others involved in doing some or all of it for you.

You also have to determine if the trainees must first have certain knowledge or skills without which they are unable to start learning your subject. A graphic example of the need for doing this is the case of a large manufacturer that sells its products overseas, particularly in Africa and the Middle East. As part of its service, the company offers intensive training to its customers who can send their staff to learn how to maintain these products. One of the instructors specializes in electronics and his role is to teach how to diagnose and fix electrical problems. He complains about the difficulty of his job because he is regularly faced with students who do not have even the basic knowledge of electronics theory, which is fundamental to his course. Unfortunately, as far as he is concerned, that is their problem and he just proceeds with his pre-arranged plans. Not surprisingly, some course participants learn very little, and this instructor does not gain much in the way of job satisfaction!

Prospective trainees must be screened for the prerequisite knowledge, and the instructor must be prepared to give a "crash course" to bring participants up to standard so the training can then proceed. Not to do so is really an exercise in futility.

To conduct a needs analysis, follow these steps:

(a) *Identify the target audience.* Who is to be trained? In general terms, what are their job responsibilities, experiences, needs, previous education/training, expectations, and, if relevant, age?

(b) *Review the relevant aspects of their particular jobs.* Identify the skills and knowledge needed now (and/or in the future) to perform the job at a reasonable and acceptable level. You also need to know about any probable changes in the work situation. It may be that new technology is being introduced into certain work areas, so you would have to decide what would be needed for performing in the new way.

(c) *Find out what the people involved feel is needed.* You can ascertain this by surveying or interviewing the actual target group (or a sample of them), their immediate supervisors/managers, or other relevant people in the organization. You can ask straightforward questions about what they believe should be learned, what improvements in performance are needed, or what problems or concerns they have that could be appropriately addressed by training.

b. DEFINE YOUR OBJECTIVES

When you have done your needs analysis, you can begin defining objectives for the training. Once you have identified, in specific terms, exactly what you want the trainees/learners to be able to do at the end of your session, you can plan how to achieve those objectives: what methods you will use, in what sequence you will present the instruction, and finally, how you will evaluate the learning/instructing.

Objectives are statements that clearly state the target or terminal performance. They specify exactly what trainees will be able to do at the end and include standards to measure trainees' performances against a minimum acceptable level of performance. These can be written in terms of specific quality, quantity, time, etc.

Objective statements also include the conditions under which learners will have to perform. These can be constraints or limitations and might include where, when, and with what (e.g., the equipment), they will do whatever is to be done.

There are three different types of objectives you might consider:

(a) *Operational objectives:* These can be measured in terms of organizational outputs such as improved productivity, reduced costs/errors, increased sales, decreased turnover.

(b) *Performance objectives:* These are related to an individual's specific job performance.

(c) *Instructional objectives:* These are written in terms of what trainees will be able to do at the end of the training session and can be evaluated by appropriate tests.

To be practical, goals must be attainable within the time limited to you. It is often more efficient to break down the goal into a series of more easily achieved steps, or objectives, rather than work on a single, long-term goal.

You also want to state your objectives precisely. Be specific and avoid using vague phrases like "to know," "to understand," "to appreciate," "to believe," "to grasp the significance of," and "to be aware of." Instead, use words like "list," "describe," "explain," "give examples of," etc.

If the vaguer terms are the first words which come to mind, simply ask yourself "What will the learner have to do to prove it?" The action word then generated will probably be much more precise.

For example, suppose you are making a presentation on stress management. The following might be your program objectives:

At the end of this program, participants will be able to —

- define stress,

- give examples of negative reactions of stress,

- list ways to overcome or minimize the adverse effects of stress,

- identify their own sources of stress in the workplace, and

- develop an action plan for managing stress more effectively.

So, to sum up, objectives are written to —

(a) set clear outcomes for both trainers and trainees;

(b) provide concrete, measurable session goals (these can be the basis for tests/evaluations);

(c) save time by helping determine just *what* should be taught and *how*;

(d) determine what existing skills, knowledge, or behaviors are essential before the new learning can start.

Remember, the objectives are what the learners will do, not what the instructor will do. If objectives are very clearly expressed, it is easier to work out how you can test the learning. In fact, it can sometimes be easier to determine the objectives by asking: "How will I test the learning? What will they have to do?"

c. MAPPING IT OUT

Whatever the type of session or meeting, it is vital to spend time on preparation and on writing down precisely what it is you are trying to achieve and how you intend to do so. By defining your objectives, you have already done the first. Now, you need to plan your strategy.

A written plan is important because it helps you organize. It enables you to see all the aspects of the lesson beforehand, to determine priorities, and to work out how best to achieve desired results, including the order of procedure, and appropriate allocation of time.

During the session, you can use your written plan as a reminder and to help keep you on track. It will also give you confidence, since you know you are prepared and do not have to worry about forgetting something. Your plan ensures that you achieve your stated objectives.

After your training session is over, you can compare the way the session went against your written plan. In this way, you can check the effectiveness of your instructional methods and techniques and your analysis may lead to improvements or changes. You will also have a record for future use which will save time and thought when you have to repeat a session.

Your session should be divided into the following phases:

(a) Introduction

(b) Main body

(c) Test of learning

(d) Conclusion

How you conduct each phase depends on what you are teaching, that is, whether you are passing information or teaching a skill.

1. Introduction

The introduction can be the most important part of your session, since it is your opportunity to grab your learners' attention and interest. If you fail to do that, the chances of the students learning what you want them to are very limited. The introduction should —

(a) motivate trainees to learn by gaining their interest as soon as possible and by giving them a purpose for learning. Explaining the benefits to them is one way to catch their attention. For example, you might explain how it will help them in their work, the future, or in the next stage of learning.

(b) forge a link with previous learning or experience. You might include a review by you or by the group so that you can check for the essential existing skills or knowledge that you identified when writing the objectives. Now you can progress from the known to the unknown.

(c) point the way ahead. Explain the goals and how they will be achieved (i.e., what methods you will use, how long different stages will take).

(d) let participants know what you expect of them. Let them know what they will have to do during, at the end of, and after the lesson.

2. The body

The body of the lesson is the main content — the new ideas and processes to be taught. In your plan, you need to decide exactly how you will teach them. To do this, you —

(a) plan your teaching points,

(b) put them in an appropriate order (i.e., from the simple to the complex, in a logical sequence), and

(c) decide the best methods and activities for gaining and maintaining the learners' attention and interest, as well as helping them to understand and learn.

For example, if you were leading a workshop in writing press releases, you might start by jotting down your teaching points as they occur to you:

(a) A press release is...

(b) A press release must include this information...

(c) Press releases are read by... and those people look for...

(d) Getting your release to the media

(e) Style

(f) Appearance

(g) The purpose of a press release is...

(h) Grammar

(i) Tips for creating attention-grabbing releases

(j) Headlines

(k) The perfect press release...

(l) What to leave out

After reviewing these, you might decided that (g) is really a point that could be covered under (a), so you eliminate it as a major division. You also add a summary at the end of the list.

You then reorganize your points into a logical order:

(a) A press release is...

(b) The perfect press release...

(c) Press releases are read by... and those people look for...

(d) A press release must include this information...

(e) Appearance

(f) Style

(g) Grammar

(h) Headlines

(i) Tips for creating attention-grabbing releases

(j) What to leave out

(k) Getting your release to the media

(l) Summary

Obviously, it makes sense to start with an introduction to the concept of press releases, and this leads logically into a discussion of who will be reading your masterpiece and what they want to see.

This outline follows a topic-oriented approach to the subject, but you could have as easily chosen a chronological approach, taking the trainee step by step through the process of creating a release. There are many ways to organize information and it is up to you to find the way that best suits your subject and audience. Whatever way you choose, be sure that you remain consistent; don't switch halfway from a step-by-step approach to a topic-oriented approach or you will throw your students off balance.

The body of the lesson should be broken into stages for easy understanding. Each stage should be confirmed before going on to the next stage and each stage should, as much as possible, be linked to the next one, as well as the one which preceded it.

If you are giving an information session, the body should include explanation, some purposeful activity or application by the trainees, and a summary. The explanation is more than just "telling." Even at this stage, you can get the trainees involved by building on existing knowledge. Get learners to think and answer questions; use any other means to elicit some of the information from them, too.

You next need to think about ways to convey your information in interesting and memorable ways. If you can find a purposeful activity to incorporate into the session, that can help the students learn by engaging their attention; this will lead to better understanding and help them to apply and remember the new information more effectively.

In the topic-oriented approach to a workshop seminar on writing press releases, you might consider three different ways of presenting the information related to each topic. For example, for (a), you might have an overhead display listing your points in the definition of a press release. For (b), you might have handouts of good and bad press releases — perhaps even a humorous "everything-gone-wrong" press release illustrating as many mistakes as possible. For (c), you might start by asking your students to talk about what they like to read in the paper or hear on the radio, then getting them to relate that to what editors look for in a press release and why, and finally, how they can fulfill the editor's and readers' expectations. To introduce (d), you could teach students a mnemonic device to help them remember the most important information that must be included in all press releases.

By incorporating a variety of techniques in this way, you keep the audience interested and alert.

Your summary can be a repetition, a review, and a link to the next element.

When teaching physical skills, the learners must obviously practice the skills. But it is also helpful to have practice time in other kinds of teaching sessions. Try to build in activities that will achieve this purpose. For example, you can design questions to challenge the trainees' new-found knowledge and allow them to discover their level of comprehension. Phrase your questions so that trainees will have to explain or give examples, not just answer yes

or no. For example, when reviewing new safety procedures, you might ask, "Joe, what would you now have to arrange differently in your work area to comply with regulation 642?"

3. Testing

The testing portion of your session should confirm what has been learned and how well it has been learned, how each student has progressed, where there are problems or areas to be reviewed or clarified, and how effective the instruction has been. This will help you make any changes or improvements in your presentation or your testing methods. The trainees will also find out what they have learned correctly and where they might need assistance, review, or practice.

For physical skills, obviously, it is most appropriate for learners to perform the skills being taught to the required standards and under the conditions already determined.

To test knowledge, information, and concepts learners must answer questions designed to discover what and how well they have learned. They can answer orally or on paper, in writing or diagrams, whatever seems the most useful. The type of test used should reflect the objectives you have established.

For example, in the press release seminar discussed above, the major objective is to enable students to write good press releases. So, the most obvious test of this would be to have them write a couple. You might provide them with a sheet of information and ask them to compose a release based on that information. Or, you might have prepared a number of fake stories that you hand out to students and then have students pair up and interview each other to glean the necessary information for a sparkling press release.

4. Conclusion

Your conclusion should always be a clear and definite end to the session. It is the final look at the session and can serve to —

(a) summarize what was taught and what was learned and, perhaps, praise individuals for successful learning,

(b) review the main points,

(c) emphasize the key aspects of the lesson,

(d) relate the different parts of the lesson to each other, and

(e) link the session to any follow-up to provide a sense of progression.

Sample #1 shows a session plan you might follow.

As you plan the lesson, you need to ask yourself both what and how you will teach.

"What" raises the question of the subject matter — not just what to include, but also what to leave out. You should limit this by deciding what, at the end, the learners *must* know; that is, what is the absolute essential minimum knowledge required.

Then move to the next level; what should the students know by the end of the lesson? What is the amount and/or depth of knowledge which can be given so that the students will gain a greater understanding of the subject? Finally, what *could* students know? What knowledge is desirable for, though not essential to, a fuller knowledge?

In deciding the level or depth of the subject matter to teach, you may be guided by the time available, but especially by the learners' capacity, how much they already know, and how quickly or easily they may learn.

Remember: it is better to teach a small amount well rather than to try to impart a lot that does not stick.

Sample #2 shows a preparation checklist you may find helpful.

"How" will include the process of the teaching and the techniques to be employed as well as the aids and equipment to be used. You will need to consider what facility is available to you and whether you have access to audiovisual material or overhead projectors, for example.

d. DEMONSTRATIONS AND PRACTICE SESSIONS

1. Task analysis

If you are leading a training session in some physical skill — perhaps learning a new computer function or maintaining a new line of photocopiers — the majority of the time should be spent in trainees practicing, with your help where needed. In this case, when you are preparing your lesson, you need to analyze the tasks or skills to be practiced and determine how your session will be structured around this practice. Demonstration and practice time will make up the body portion of your session plan.

It is helpful to perform the task yourself before the session so that you can break it down into steps or stages and describe the steps as key points. *Steps* or stages are suitable portions of a task for learners to master. Avoid overloading and look for the ends of the various operations, points in the task where you change from doing one thing to another, or where one part has been fitted to another. Make sure there are not too many stages (probably not more than seven).

Key points are the vital elements of each stage that the learners must remember if they are to perform the task correctly. They can include factors that affect quality or safety, aid in remembering, make the work easier to do, or any other special information. Limit key points to four or less in any one stage.

Sample #3 shows how teaching people a simple operation of running a microwave oven can be broken down into steps and key points.

2. Demonstrations

If you plan to introduce your practice time with a demonstration, be sure you separate the two functions clearly. At no time during

1. **Instructional objectives:**
   (Including performance, standards, and conditions of performance)
   At the end of this lesson, students will be able to:

   - List and describe the 4 parts of the Food Guide

   - Plan an appropriate daily meal plan using the key elements (and servings) of the Food Guide.

2. **Prerequisite knowledge and/or skills:**
   Before they can start this lesson, students must be able to:

   1. Define nutrition
   2. Give reasons for maintaining "healthy" weight

3. **Introduction:**
   LINK to previous learning/experience: Previous learning about nutrition — Ask them to define and explain
   - What most people mean by "diet" — they explain

   GOALS of today's lesson:

   Learn what should comprise a nutritional "diet"

   PURPOSE for today's learning (e.g., for next stage/work/future):

   Be able to plan and eat well and guide others to do so.

   OTHER "attention-grabber," motivation, etc:

   Perhaps lose weight (if needed), feel better

4.   **Main body: (Note: WHAT will be taught, and HOW)**

Teaching Point	Activity: Teacher/Student	Time
#1 Overview of 4 groups of Food Guide	ask them for names " " for examples (Give examples if they don't know)	15 mins.
#2 Go through each group in detail	They give examples; teacher adds	15 mins.
#3 The Menu	Students plan 1 day - groups of 3	20 mins.

5.   **Test of learning:**

They summarize groups (without help) and plan menus for a day. (Go through)

6.   **Conclusion:**

SUMMARY of LESSON: Go through groups and examples

EMPHASIS of KEY POINTS:

O.H.T. of names and need for each

WHAT NEXT:

They plan a healthy menu for 1 week.

Subject: *Nutrition*   **Topic:** *Food Guide*

Session plan number: *3*   **Time allocation:** *1 1/2 hours*

Session objective: At the end of this session, students/trainees will be able to:

1. *List and describe the 4 parts of the Food Guide*

2. *Plan a daily menu to include requisite servings from each group.*

Facility to be used: *Room #3*

Set-up/room arrangement required: *U-shaped or tables*

Materials and equipment: (specify which participants must bring)

1. *Text book*
2. *Paper + pens*
3. _____
4. _____
5. _____
6. _____

AUDIOVISUAL AIDS:
Equipment:

1. *overhead projector*
2. *Screen*
3. _____
4. _____

Items: (e.g., name/# films or videos)

1. O.H.T.s from file [1-6]
2. Blank O.H.T.s + pens
3. Chart #2
4.

Printed matter (books for reference, manuals, notes, forms)

1. Text book
2. Menu forms
3.
4.

Handout materials:

1. Booklet - Food Guide
2.
3.
4.

Special research: (for instructor)

Preparatory assignment for participants: (e.g., reading, projects, assignments)

Chapter 2 in textbook

Assignment for participants after the session:

They plan 1 week menu

USING THE MICROWAVE OVEN FOR TIME COOKING: "TWO-STAGE COOKING"

STEPS or STAGES	KEY POINTS
Select cooking power by pressing or tapping continuously POWER control.	Clock time disappears. Selected Power indicator light turns on.
Set cooking time by continuously pressing or tapping TIME controls.	Temperature probe must not be connected to oven wall receptacle during programming time because it will cancel the time setting. Cooking time appears in display window in minutes and seconds.
Select second cooking power by pressing continuously or tapping POWER control.	Previously selected time and power indicator light disappear from display window. Second stage power indicator light turns on.
Set second stage cooking time by pressing continuously or tapping TIME controls.	Second stage cooking time appears in display window.
Touch START button.	Oven light turns on. Cooking begins and goes through two steps; then oven turns off. Time of day shows in display window.

this part of the session should learners be allowed to perform the skill at the same time as you are demonstrating. They must concentrate totally on what you are doing so that they recognize how the skill is done correctly.

The demonstration sequence is as follows:

(a) Show, at roughly normal speed, how to perform the skill to be learned.

(b) Demonstrate the whole task, slowly, step by step, explaining it very clearly and carefully. From time to time, try to make eye contact with the trainees to check for non-verbal signs of understanding, or lack of understanding. This stage may be repeated for more complex tasks and if there are problems in understanding.

(c) Now demonstrate the task again, this time with the learners giving each step and the key points for the instructor to follow. This provides immediate evidence about the level of learners' understanding, showing whether they are now ready to practice the skill or whether they need clarification or repetition. It means you do not have to ask the rather useless question: "Do you understand?" You will obviously check their real understanding at this stage.

3. Practice

Participants in the training session should begin practicing the skill only when you are sure that they have a clear concept of what they are trying to do. Provide help where needed and as soon as possible so that they can practice doing it correctly and not develop bad habits. Allow time for participants to continue to practice under supervision so they increase accuracy, speed, and performance levels.

If many learners seem to have difficulties in performing the task, or have any misapprehension, you should stop the practice and demonstrate the correct performance of the skill again. Let them resume practicing when you are sure they are ready to do so and previous difficulties have been resolved. In any group, there will be individual differences in the speed and ease with which participants learn. You will have to show patience and encourage the slower learners, being as positive as you can.

At least 50% of the total time should be allocated to the practice portion of the session since this is the most crucial part. Remember: we learn by doing.

e. GETTING IT ON PAPER

1. Getting started

If you are having trouble marshalling your thoughts at the planning stage, the best way to overcome this is to start writing whatever you can. Do not try for perfection or worry about a finished plan. It is often helpful to begin by brainstorming with yourself: just write down any words, phrases, and ideas, at random, as they occur to you. Do not worry, yet, about order. You may then note main points, headings, key words, facts, anecdotes, as well as audio-visual aids. You might even put this aside for a while and come back to it later.

It may be helpful to plan your opening and ending, perhaps write your first and last sentences. Try to grab attention immediately: use an important fact or a relevant story, for example. Lead with your ace, for example, the seriousness of the situation. Give figures or a startling statement, or a question for trainees to answer or consider.

2. The five Ws

Asking yourself Who, What, Where, When, Why (and How) will help you organize your program.

(a) Why am I giving this presentation?

There may be one or more reasons for your presentation:

- To inform or instruct

- To persuade or sell

- To make recommendations and gain acceptance

- To arouse interest

- To inspire or initiate action

- To evaluate, interpret, and clarify

- To set the stage for further action

- To gather and explore ideas

Write a specific objective to help you visualize the end of the talk in terms of what you want to happen and what the audience will do or take with them at the end.

(b) Who is going to be there?

Try to get a list of participants' names and titles (and roles if possible) and ask for any relevant information about them. If possible, talk to them first (remember your needs analysis). Find out about their existing knowledge and experience, their familiarity with the subject, their interests and attitudes, and even if they are likely to be on your side or not.

(c) What am I going to say?

To help you decide what you are going to say, ask yourself questions such as: what do they already know and what do they want to know? What do they need to know in what detail, background, level? What don't they need to know, that is, what can I or should I leave out and what should I avoid talking about? What handouts would be helpful and how many copies will I need?

(d) Where will it take place?

Make sure that the room is booked and is appropriate in terms of the size, shape, and facilities provided. Find out what is available there, such as equipment, help, heat and ventilation, seats and seating arrange-

ment. Is it comfortable, can you arrange it in the way best suited to your purpose?

(e) When will it take place?

You need to consider timing very carefully. Consider precisely when the presentation will take place: the day of the week, the day of the month, and the time of day, as well as the length and duration. If you can, avoid traditionally poor times for seminars or presentations: just before or after lunch, or at the very end of the day.

Most adults are more attentive in the morning and this is generally the best time for meetings where keen concentration is necessary. This would be true for picking up new knowledge and information, for problem solving, and, especially, for one-way communication methods like lectures.

There is usually a period of lowered concentration after meals while food is digested and there is also a "down" time just before lunch, say, when people are feeling hungry and their blood sugar levels are low. The evening is usually the least desirable time, especially if it is a continuation of the day session or it follows a day's work. It is important to vary the pace and the methods used at different times of day to accommodate these factors.

If participants are feeling work pressures it will affect their concentration. For instance, if an organization's financial year-end is coming up and everyone is rushing to draw up financial statements and get budgets prepared, those involved might not want to take time out to attend any training or other meetings that they do not feel are as important at this particularly busy time.

Will longer sessions be held over consecutive days versus, say, one day a week for a few weeks? There are several advantages to running over consecutive days; often it is easier for individuals to form into a "group" or a team with a sense of common purpose. The information and knowledge usually transfers more coherently and you can gain momentum and build on what has already been achieved without having to review as much as if there are longer breaks between sessions. The majority of people prefer this option, since a sense of completion is more quickly reached and it is less likely that unknown factors will prevent attendance once the initial arrangements have been made. It may be difficult for staff to be released for two or more consecutive days, however, so the second option may be the only one. On the positive side, the one-day-a-week option allows time between sessions for coming up with new ideas, for ideas to "sink in," and for applying or trying out what has been learned.

Are people giving up their own time, whether it is before or after work, on the weekend, or during their vacation? If so, are they are being given time off to compensate? Their level of motivation and interest can easily be affected by the amount of personal choice about attending during their own time. If the organization insists on disrupting private time, this sends a message about their concern for their staff and, if it is training that is being given, their commitment to training.

(f) How am I going to do it?

Plan and organize your presentation to achieve your purpose and enlist help that might be available to you at any stage.

3. Note-writing

When you first make your notes, you will probably end up with many pages of what looks rather like a long essay. This should only be your starting point, since it is inadvisable to have such a document as your end product.

It is certainly a good idea to have notes to refer to, but you only want them as a reference. If you look as though you are reading straight off the paper, you will lose credibility. On the other hand, never attempt to memorize a presentation or talk.

This puts too much pressure on you; it is easy to blank out and a memorized presentation can sound false.

You will soon find that if you do your homework, prepare well, and stay organized, you will have the confidence to make your presentation from your notes without worrying about memorizing everything. Take these steps to organize your notes and draft your presentation:

(a) Put your notes in order: first your introduction, then the body, and then the conclusion.

(b) Flesh out the body of your presentation by making a skeleton outline and then creating sections and subsections.

(c) Make a rough draft and add in pertinent facts, figures, appropriate phrases, and words. Consider the words you will use; use concrete, familiar, specific (perhaps dramatic) words.

(d) Add in your examples, illustrations, and the places where you need audiovisuals. Start to plan the audiovisual aids; what will you use and how.

Now you are ready to revise and simplify your rough draft. Avoid full sentences; they make your notes long and this makes it harder for you to refer briefly to your notes and find what you are looking for. If you know what you are talking about, main words and point form will probably be enough and you will be quite able to form your own sentences when you are talking. Put key words or points on the left with secondary points to the right.

Sample #4 shows how session notes can be organized. If you are running a session that will be longer than a few hours, perhaps a two-day workshop or two-session seminar, you will also find it helpful to plan a daily activity schedule such as the one shown in Sample #5. The activity schedule will help you plan what you will do, how you will do it, and how long each section will take. (Seminars and workshops are discussed in more detail in chapter 4.)

Think of your notes as your script; it should be written for content plus "stage directions" for you. Ensure visibility by making your notes in large print or large type and well spaced. I suggest printing as opposed to ordinary writing because printing is easier for you to read, and most of us usually print larger and clearer than we write.

Use any techniques that will make your script more visible and memorable. For example, use —

- colored pens (you might devise a color code or system)

- underlining

- boxes around items

- asterisks

- marks to remind you where to pause, emphasize, make special gestures

- marks to remind you where, when, and how long to use any audio-visual aids, handouts, etc.

Number the pages clearly, use one side only, and do not staple pages together. This will enable you to put pages down when you have finished with them and not rustle sheets as you turn them. (Another useful tip is to hold these notes in your nondominant hand, that is, your left if you are right-handed. We tend to gesture more with the dominant hand, so we're more likely to distract an audience by waving around notes held in this hand, and also risk dropping them.)

I advise using paper rather than small cards: I have witnessed the embarrassment of speakers dropping small cards and then having to scrabble around to collect them again!

f. EVALUATION

You may think of evaluation as what you and/or the trainees do at the end of training or after a presentation has been made. However, it is better to decide *ahead of time* how you plan to evaluate any session or program, and then when, how often, and by whom evaluation should take place.

There are four basic ways to evaluate training:

(a) *Reaction:* What was the trainees' immediate reaction? Were they satisfied with the program in terms of content and how it was presented?

(b) *Learning:* What knowledge, skills, techniques did they actually learn? It is important to ask questions (either on a written questionnaire or face to face) to find out whether the session achieved its goals, whether they learned anything and, if so, what? This means asking about the specific knowledge or skills you attempted to communicate — not just about the general emotional reaction to the session.

(c) *Behavior:* What changes were there which then improved work performance? This can be assessed by follow-up back in their work setting, by the trainees, their managers, and their colleagues. If changes in attitude are a desired outcome of the training, these should be expressed as specific behaviors so that they can be checked afterwards. (Note that this type of follow-up testing is more appropriate for smaller training sessions when you are able to return to the work setting and talk to participants and supervisors. If you are running a session at which participants from out-of-town are attending — perhaps as part of a regional conference — this may not be feasible.)

Name of session		Audiovisuals
INTRODUCTION:		
KEY WORD 1.		
Balanced diet - food	Point (a) weight	Trans. #1
	Point (b) nutrition	
	Point (c) Food Guide	
MAIN BODY:		
KEY WORD 1.		
Fruits and vegetables	Point (a) examples and best choices	Trans. #2
	Point (b) no. of servings	
	Point (c)	
KEY WORD 2.		
Breads and cereals	Point (a) examples	
	Point (b) no. of servings	Trans. #3
	Point (c)	
KEY WORD 3.		
Dairy	Point (a) examples	
	Point (b) no. of servings	
	Point (c)	
KEY WORD 4.		
Meat, fish, etc.	Point (a) examples	Handout #1
	Point (b) servings	
	Point (c) alternates	
SUMMARY:		
KEY WORD 1. Food Guide points		Trans. #4
KEY WORD 2. nutrition		
KEY WORD 3. diet		
KEY WORD 4.		
CONCLUSION:		
KEY WORD Balanced		Handout #2

The Supervisor's Role in Health and Safety
Activity Schedule:

Day 1 — Morning:

Introductions: to self, program, objectives, each other	9:00 — 9:30
Small Group Discussion:	9:30 — 10:00

- The role of the supervisor in safety
- Common safety problems at work

Report back, Discuss, Summary	10:00 — 10:30
Break	10:30 — 10:45
Leader Input + Discussion, Summary	10:45 — noon

- The new health and safety laws

Lunch	12:00 — 1:00

Afternoon:

Case Study #1:	1:00 — 2:00

- Small Group Discussion/Problem-solving 1:00 — 2:00
- Report back with Discussion 2:00 — 2:45
- Summary of Key Points 2:45 — 3:00

Break	3:00 — 3:15
Introduce, Show film #1, Discuss	3:15 — 4:00
Explain Evening Assignment &	
Summary Wrap-up	4:00 — 4:15

(d) *Results:* Did the program produce the results the organization wanted (e.g., reduced costs, improved productivity)?

Sample #6 shows an evaluation chart to help you plan your session by thinking WHO you will get your feedback from (sources of information), HOW you will collect the information, and WHAT potential problems might arise. From this chart, you can develop an evaluation questionnaire. For example, if you determine that most of your information will come from participants directly during the time of the session, you might eliminate a written evaluation and rely on face-to-face feedback.

When designing your evaluation questionnaires, bear in mind that anonymity is often preferable because you are more likely to get honest reactions. There is also less worry about confidentiality and most of the time it matters little whether you can identify writers.

For rating scales, use an even number (say from 1 to 4), or an even number of categories or words to avoid the tendency to mark straight down the middle. Make it easy for people to answer. For immediate reactions, you will probably want feedback on the following:

(a) Background information (e.g., was this session voluntarily attended or not? Was there sufficient information about the program beforehand?)

(b) Program objectives

(c) Relevance

(d) Program design (e.g., content, organization, format, timing, and duration)

(e) Instructional techniques, methods, and materials

(f) Evaluation of the instructor

(g) Facility and its suitability

(h) Other comments

Sample #7 shows an evaluation questionnaire for trainees to record their immediate reactions and Sample #8 shows a follow-up questionnaire for trainees after they've had a chance to use their new skills.

g. SUMMARY

Now you have your basic outline in place, measure it against these dictums. To be successful, any training must —

(a) Support the goals and objectives of the employer organization. An effective needs assessment should ensure that training is planned for achieving the purposes of the organization.

(b) Contribute to productivity and high quality of job performance. A job analysis can determine the human, technical, and process aspects of job performance.

(c) Be measurable. Written objectives should state the specific performance to be achieved and the standards and conditions under which it will be performed.

(d) Be competently delivered in order to achieve its intention.

(e) Be evaluated to ensure that it did accomplish what was intended.

SAMPLE #6
TRAINING EVALUATION CHART

What might be measured	Sources of information	How information will be collected	Potential problems
1. REACTION	Participants	- evaluation form - speaker assessment	- must ask right questions
2. LEARNING	Participant/Instructor	- Evaluation during practice - Feedback and questionnaires	Time
3. BEHAVIOR	Self (Participant) - Manager - Colleagues - Client/customer	Questionnaires Interviews	- Time - ensuring get returns of questionnaires
4. RESULTS	Manager Budgets	Questionnaire/ Interview	Design reporting sheets

Program Evaluation

Program name: _Assertiveness in the Workplace_

Date: _January 12, 199–_   Instructor: _Mary Lamb_

We appreciate your feedback and comments about the training program you have attended.

Please circle the response which best describes your reactions:

1 = Strongly agree   2 = Agree   3 = Disagree   4 = Strongly disagree

1. I was keen to attend this program   ① 2 3 4

2. The content was what I expected   1 ② 3 4

3. I received sufficient information ahead of time   1 2 ③ 4

4. My program objectives were:
    (a) _How to deal with rude people_   1 ② 3 4
    (b) _Getting co-operation with colleagues, staff_   1 ② 3 4
    (c) _Handling criticism_   ① 2 3 4
    (d) _Saying "no"_   ① 2 3 4

    These objectives were met. (Please respond for each objective you wrote down.)

5. The length of the program was appropriate   1 2 ③ 4

6. The program was aimed at the appropriate level   1 ② 3 4

7. I learned something new which was of value   1 ② 3 4

8. There was sufficient practice and exercise with new skills and concepts   1 2 ③ 4

9. Handouts and written materials were useful   ① 2 3 4

10. Audiovisual materials were used effectively   ① 2 3 4

11. Sufficient time was allowed for discussion   1 ② 3 4

12. There was good use of different methods   1 ② 3 4

13. The program leader was knowledgeable   ① 2 3 4

14. The program leader was well organized   ① 2 3 4

15. The presentation was clear and understandable   ① 2 3 4

16. The program leader held my interest and attention   ① 2 3 4

17. The program leader was flexible to group needs   ① 2 3 4

18. What I found of most value was:

   Good use of visual aids and handouts,
     also real examples

19. My suggestions for changes and/or improvements:

   Longer program, with more opportunity
     to practice skills

20. Other comments:

   Please give a follow-up session (see #19.)
     with same instruction.

SAMPLE #8
FOLLOW-UP PROGRAM EVALUATION

Program: _Time Management_   Date attended: _March 9, 199—_

Program Leader: _Jane Smart_

(a) To be completed by participant

1. What I learned from this program:

   (a) Precisely where I need to improve!

   (b) Some ideas skills to use

   (c) Where it's the situation I can't control

2. The program helped me improve in the following areas:

   Prioritizing my workload better — daily and longer

3. I have managed to apply the following in my work setting:

   "To do" list, more planning time

4. I have not managed to apply the following:

   Reorganizing my filing system to improve this area

   "Quiet time"

5. What was most valuable was:

   - Questionnaires
   - Handouts - worksheets for use at work
   - Film

6. What was least valuable was:

   Discussion on delegation: I have no one to delegate to...

7. My comments/ suggestions now about this program:

   Have a follow-up discussion session where we can discuss problems <u>now</u> and how to deal with them.

(b) To be completed by participant's supervisor/manager

As a result of attending the program, this participant:

1. Has learned the following skills/concepts:

    Where he needs to improve and some techniques for this

2. Has improved in the following areas:

    Prioritizing regular workload

3. Has managed to apply:

    Techniques ; Priorities ; Communicating with me ; Writing down more about workload needs

4. Still has needs in the area of:

    Handling sudden switches of priorities

5. My comments/suggestions about this program now:

    Longer ; follow up with assignment between sessions .

3 *Putting out the welcome mat*

No matter what your topic or who your audience, participants in your workshop or seminar should feel comfortable — both physically and emotionally. If people arrive late because they have had trouble finding the venue, feeling hassled because it is being held at an inconvenient time, under- or overdressed because they haven't been properly informed about appropriate attire, or unprepared because no one told them they were supposed to bring a work-in-progress for discussion, for example, you're going to have a much more difficult time winning them over and successfully communicating your topic.

You want to do everything you can to set the climate for learning. In a proper learning environment, participants will have a positive attitude toward —

(a) you and the information you are presenting, and

(b) the client group or their organization.

a. FIRST IMPRESSIONS COUNT

Most people attending a seminar or workshop have an attitude — good or bad — towards the situation before you even have a chance to say "Good morning." For example, if Fran is being forced to attend your seminar on customer service and telephone etiquette because her boss has told her she is too abrupt with clients, she may feel threatened or even embarrassed. On the other hand, if answering the phone and talking directly to clients is a new and exciting step up in Fran's responsibilities, she may have a very positive attitude and look forward to learning new things.

You may have no control over the attitude that participants bring to your session. You *do* have control over the impression that you provide to participants about yourself and the session. It is to your advantage to provide participants with as much information as possible about yourself, the program, the benefits of attending, and what is expected of them. If you can provide this information a few days before the session begins, so much the better. Win them over with your credentials, your planning and organization, and your friendly, professional tone. In an advance information package, you might suggest appropriate dress, include clear instructions — perhaps even a map — for reaching the venue, indicate choices of transportation, parking, etc.

It is important to be organized and ready when participants arrive at the meeting place. You want to be able to greet everyone in a friendly way rather than worrying about last-minute changes to room arrangements, whether your notes are in order, or when the coffee will arrive. I like to have a list of everyone attending, including some information about each of them, so that when I meet a participant for the first time, I am able to sound as though I am expecting him or her, personally. For example, if you know that somebody has come from another city, you might comment about that, ask about the journey, or mention if others have come from the same place. You might tell them where they can put their outdoor clothes and the location of the washrooms. It is often very welcoming to offer some refreshments at the start.

This greeting and chatting time is not only pleasant for the participants, but it also helps to relax you and make you feel that the group is more than a collection of strangers. Be sure to leave a few moments in your program for this introductory and settling stage. While participants will expect and appreciate the session to start on time, they will not want to be herded into their seats before they have had time to take off their coats, get a cup of coffee, and settle in.

b. THE ROOM ARRANGEMENT

Prepare well in advance for the best room arrangement possible. Whatever room arrangement you choose, try to make the atmosphere pleasant. Try pleasant music playing softly in the background until you are ready to begin. Hand out name badges for participants to wear; this will help everyone get to know each other. Find out how participants prefer being addressed; William Smith might prefer Bill or Will for example. Don't forget to consider temperature, ventilation, and lighting when setting up the room.

The various common styles of room arrangement each serve a different purpose and are described below.

1. Theater style

The theater-style setup is similar to that found in a regular theater (or cinema) — hence its name. The many rows of seats are usually fixed and all face the front, sometimes in tiers or banks, across the full width of the room. The speaker stands at the front, facing the group (see Figure #1).

This style is commonly used for conferences and in large auditoriums or lecture theaters. It is more appropriate for large groups, for a more lecture-style presentation, and is much better if the seating is banked, and/or you stand on a raised platform, stage, or dais, so that you can see the audience better, and they can all see you easily.

FIGURE #1
ROOM ARRANGEMENT — THEATER STYLE

FIGURE #2
ROOM ARRANGEMENT — CLASSROOM STYLE

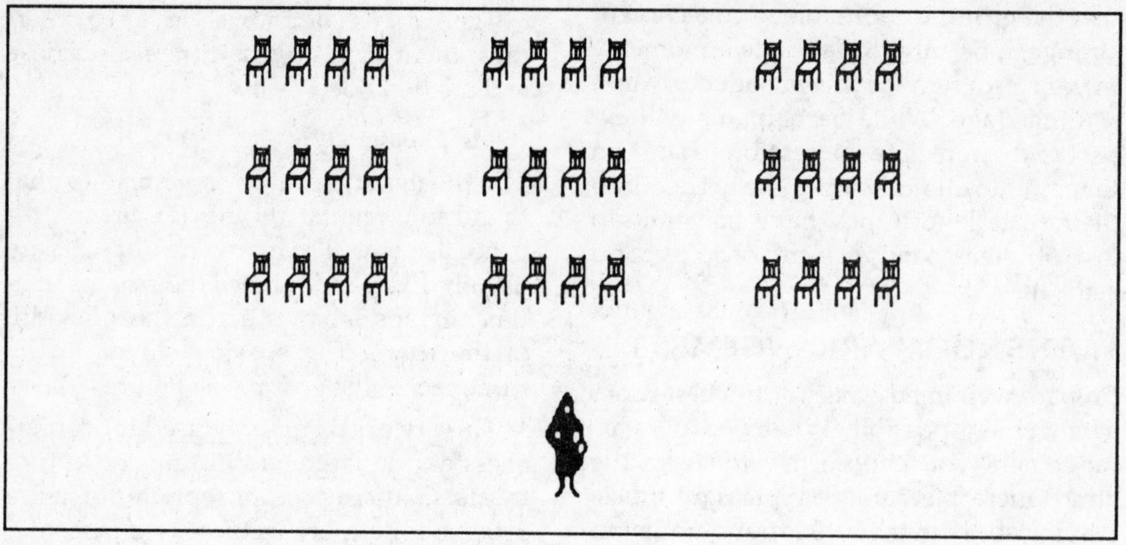

Participation can be limited in this arrangement, particularly between those attending since they cannot easily see the faces of many of the other participants. Nevertheless, you can encourage involvement if you wish, by having small discussion groups of three or four people, comprising those sitting next to each other in the same row. Chances are that most groups would contain people who knew each other, since, in settings like these, people tend to sit next to friends and colleagues. For more mixed groups and more interest, you can have the groups made up of two from one row and two from the row in front turning around to talk to them.

You can also invite questions and comments during or at the conclusion of your presentation. This question period will increase participation and interest and provide you with some feedback. Make sure everyone has heard the question asked before you respond.

2. Classroom style

In a classroom style, there are fewer and shorter rows, sometimes with tables in front of each place (see Figure #2). This arrangement often has the effect of reminding people of previous school experiences, which may not be positive. Also, they may have expectations and feelings about the "leader" based on their former teachers.

With this style, group participation is not easy unless you move the chairs around. Again, as in theater style, you must also be aware of those who choose to sit at the back since you might have difficulty drawing them in.

3. Boardroom or U-shape

Longer tables can be arranged in a U-shape with participants sitting around the outside of three sides so all can face the front of the room where the speaker is placed. A square or rectangular boardroom table can be used the same way (see Figure #3).

This style is useful for a group of up to about 30, depending on the size of the room. Nobody sits at the back, and everyone can see each other. Having each person's name printed on a large card on the table in front of them helps you and the other members of the group, too.

More involvement and participation is likely in this setup, and you need not be distant from anyone since you can walk around easily. I prefer an open or hollow section in the middle (as in the illustration) which I can walk into and get even closer to everyone

4. Small tables

Even with large groups, you can create a less-formal atmosphere and get more participation by having the group split up and seated at smaller tables around the room.

If you want to have people who do not know each other well at each table, you can have participants arrange themselves in this way, or you can set out name cards at each table. This latter method can also be used if you want to organize each group around a particular mix of people because of, for example, their background, experience, or roles.

In this setup, it is easy for you to move around and talk to everyone and be more accessible.

c. INTRODUCTIONS AND ANNOUNCEMENTS

Take the time to make introductory announcements to provide any needed information and to set the tone for the session.

1. Welcome the group

Your welcome is an important component to the first impression you make on the participants because it is your first activity in front of the whole group. Put forth a positive image; be sincere, smiling, and friendly. This makes for a great start and creates an impression that stays with everyone.

A straightforward, confident welcome always works. For example, you can simply say, "On behalf of XYZ Corporation, I wish to welcome you to our two-day program on the Essentials of Front-line Supervision. I hope you find the sessions worthwhile and productive."

2. Introduce yourself

Next, formally introduce yourself, even if you have already met some of the

FIGURE #3
ROOM ARRANGEMENT — U-SHAPE

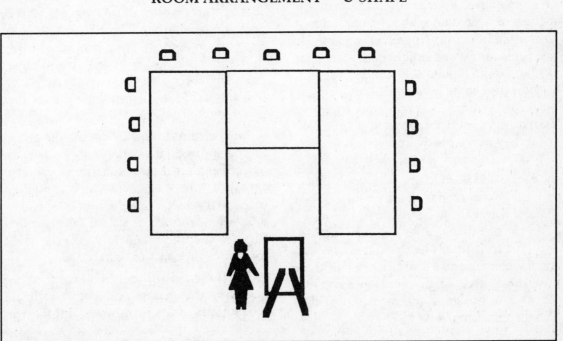

FIGURE #4
ROOM ARRANGEMENT — SMALL TABLES

participants and information about you was included in the materials they have already received. This is a time to establish, or re-establish, your credibility. You can include a few points about your educational background (if this is expected), your relevant work experience, your particular qualifications for conducting this session, and some personal details, as you wish, to be more "human" and friendly. You do not want to repeat too much of what they may already know.

If someone else has the job of welcoming the group and introducing you, you should provide that person with the specific information you want to be given. In this case, express your thanks after the introduction and add to it briefly with your own personal welcome and a few other details that you think are worth mentioning. This serves as a bridge to the next part of the initial announcements.

3. Outline the program

Briefly go through the general aims and, perhaps, specific objectives of the session. It is best to display these on a visual aid, such as an overhead projector, and limit them to ten at most. For a program lasting more than one day, give the overall objectives, then break these down for each day. It is a good idea to start each day with a statement of that day's objectives.

You can add to this by asking the group or the individual participants to list the objectives that they want the program to satisfy. Trainees can write them down on their own note pads, which you look at as you walk around, or you might ask that they tell them to the group so you can list them on a flipchart or on a board.

This exercise will help you confirm the needs of the group and could indicate which parts of the program to emphasize, which to spend more time on, and which, perhaps, to play down.

4. Outline the agenda

Let the participants know the agenda for the session; what will be included and when, how it will take place, timing, and breaks. You might want to prepare a written agenda and hand it out to the participants at this time.

Be careful to follow any agenda that you have stated because participants are likely to check it periodically. If you do have to deviate from it, say so when this happens.

5. Orientation

Briefly describe where participants can find washrooms, public telephones, eating areas, coat rooms, etc. If your session is taking place in a conference center, hotel, or other location that is used to having on-site seminars, ask the management if a map is available that you can distribute to your participants. Let them know if there is a no-smoking policy for the session. Some options are providing smoking breaks where they can step outside, leaving part of the room for smokers only and another part for non-smokers, or having a strict non-smoking policy.

By providing this kind of orientation, you show that you care about the participants as human beings and want to make them feel comfortable. And remember, the more comfortable the trainees feel, the better they are able to learn.

6. Introduce the participants

There are various ways to help everyone get to know everyone else. In a smaller group, participants can introduce themselves or you can use some of the icebreaker activities suggested below. Your choice will depend on what you wish to accomplish. Do you simply want to get to know who is attending, or do you need in-depth information about each of them in order to establish a particular mood?

Keep in mind that many people do not really like introducing themselves, feeling that they are in the spotlight. They may rush through their introduction quickly, saying little, or ramble on. If this is a concern to you, again, you can help them along by asking each person to, for example, tell three things about themselves: their name, their job title (if appropriate), and why they are attending the seminar.

d. BREAKING THE ICE

Icebreakers or warm-ups are activities designed to help create a more informal atmosphere (when appropriate) and to make participants feel more comfortable with you and with each other. It is the beginning of the networking process and of melding the individuals into a group. They are particularly useful with people who do not know each other, do not know each other well, or might be feeling somewhat apprehensive about what is going to happen.

I have already mentioned getting the participants involved by asking them to name or list their objectives. You can also elicit their expectations, which can be written up on a board or overhead projector.

Following are instructions and sample forms for two of the most popular icebreakers. There are many good books written solely on group activities and icebreakers, so you might want to check your local library. (For more icebreaking ideas, see Appendix 1.)

1. "I'd like you to meet..."

Ask participants to pair up with someone who is either unknown, or someone with whom they do not usually have a great deal of contact. (If there is an uneven number of people, have one threesome work together.) Then give them 10 minutes to take turns doing "mini-interviews," so each can get to know his or her partner. You can have the pairs do this exercise verbally or each partner can complete a Partner Introduction Form, shown in Sample #9. At the end of the allotted time, each pair can introduce each other to the group, passing on some of the details they have just discovered and feel are of interest.

This exercise ensures that everyone knows at least one other person and other members of the group will probably hear information that will stimulate interest in making contact with certain other individuals. This warm-up works better with smaller groups; it is less effective at larger seminars where participants are sitting theater-style and less able to move freely.

2. Getting to know you

Provide each participant with a sheet of paper with various categories or topics listed. Tell participants that they have 10 minutes to fill in the sheet by getting as many different people's names next to each category as they can. To accomplish this, participants will have to mingle immediately, talk to as many of the others as possible, and ask pertinent questions. Sample #10 shows a sheet that you can adapt for your own needs.

You might also use a humorous short film or video presentation to introduce the seminar or "break the ice." Humorous videos are especially effective, for example, those starring the Muppets. I have used John Cleese's two-minute film "Why Do We Work?" which is a satire on motivation.

If you want to find out what might work for you, you can get catalogs and recommendations from film libraries or companies that rent them out. You can usually preview the films or videos at no cost.

Be aware that the showing of an entire video may constitute a "public performance" of the work under copyright law and you may require the permission of the copyright holder. The rental companies and film libraries should be able to provide you with the specifics on copyright, permissions, etc.

(See section **k.** in chapter 5 for more on copyright.)

e. DEVELOPING RAPPORT

During your presentation, you want to establish the sort of relationship with individuals and the group that helps the two-way communication process. As we have previously discussed, first impressions are important and can set the tone for the session.

Everyone wants to feel they are unique individuals, so it helps to use individuals' names when speaking to them or answering their questions. If you have trouble remembering people's names, make sure you make use of name tags.

It is only professional to treat everybody with courtesy and dignity, even if they are not very polite themselves! It is important to pay attention to their needs for both physical and psychological comfort. You should show that you want to help everyone understand or learn. Your attitude of accessibility will be clear if you are approachable, welcome contributions, and show your concern in the way you handle questions and answers.

When you are in the position of instructing people, it is also important to handle errors sensitively and with tact. Many people have previously had bad experiences with the results of making mistakes. Because they may be worried about appearing foolish, they may try to avoid putting themselves in a situation where this could happen, or they might try to hide any errors. You need to allow, and even encourage, risk taking, since this is the way we learn — by taking a chance. Always point out first what the participant has already achieved, however little, rather than what he or she has done wrong. Then you can offer help, with corrections.

f. POSITIVE REINFORCEMENT

Positive reinforcement means giving a reward of any type for a particular behavior to encourage more of that behavior. There are different ways of rewarding behavior and they vary in their value for individuals.

These are typical positive responses that you might want to incorporate into your session:

(a) Verbal praise through words like good, excellent, very interesting

(b) Non-verbal responses, such as smiles and nods

(c) Repeating good answers or comments

(d) Grades or marks, where appropriate

(e) Asking for a particular contribution when you know that the individual has something special to offer in terms of experience, expertise, or ideas

Remember, however, that giving your attention itself can be rewarding, so you need to be careful not to reward any undesirable behavior by paying too much attention to it.

Positive reinforcement is often only given for good results, but people get turned off if they are immediately told they are wrong and the immediate response is "no." Use positive reinforcement for effort, too. Individuals need to feel able to take a risk and to try, knowing that they may be wrong, but they will not be made to feel or look stupid; they are much more likely to learn this way.

Organizations often give positive reinforcement to their staff by providing —

● money for taking and passing courses, or other financial support,

● special recognition, e.g., employee of the month, or

● promotion or advancement.

It is always good reinforcement to let people know when their performance or behavior has improved or when their knowledge has increased as a result of taking a course. However you choose to recognize participants, keep in mind that any reward has to be regarded as positive by the person receiving it. You might think it rewarding to ask a participant to make a special contribution to your seminar, but that person might just regard it as extra work!

Complete the following by finding out about your partner:

Name: Jacquie

Employer and type of organization: Acme Supply Co. (medical supplies)

Job position: Exec. Secretary Sales Dept.   Time in this position: 3 yrs.

Main responsibilities: Manage calendars of bosses; Administrative support; word processing; Customer service on phone

Previous experience: Customer Service Clerk Medical Secretary

Most challenging part of the job: Dealing with 4 bosses! Handling customer problems on the phone

Some personal details: She breeds championship dogs!

Other interesting facts about this person: Also has own business editing and desk top publishing.

SAMPLE #10
GETTING TO KNOW YOU

Try to find at least one person who fits each category

Name

Worked here more than three years   Vida, Roger, Stan, Diana, Stefan, Jamie, Jose

Supervise two or more staff   Diana, Jose, Vida

Commute by car   Diana, Val, Jose, Stan, Carmen, Chris

Commute by public transport   Stefan, Jamie, Roger, Vida, Marian, Boris

Play sports: squash / tennis / racquetball   Boris, Stefan, Jamie, Diana

Do aerobics / jog regularly   Stan, Boris, Diana

Married with children   Diana, Jose, Boris

Have a pet: dog / cat / other   Marian, Vida, Stefan

Wear glasses   Vida, Stan, Jamie

Wear contact lenses   Carmen, Roger

Like gourmet cooking   Roger

Drink coffee   Jose, Stan, Vida, Roger, Diana, Jamie, Carmen, Val, Boris, Stefan

Drink tea   Roger, Marian

Enjoy theater   Marian, Roger, Val, Carmen

4 Delivering your message with finesse

You've got your outlines, you know when, where, and why you are holding your workshop or seminar, and you've thought about how those first crucial moments are going to set the tone. What are some of the considerations of your method of delivery? How do you keep a lecture alive? When is the best time to use discussion groups? And how do you handle difficult questions? This chapter addresses these and other questions.

a. THE LECTURE

The lecture has been the traditional way to pass on information, especially to large groups, and it is still widely used in many educational institutions and in professional settings.

The word lecture is derived from the Latin verb, *legere,* to read, and a *lectern* is often provided to hold the notes from which the lecturer can do just that — read! This type of delivery, of course, can be deadly. Many lectures and talks overuse the channels of speaking and listening and are ineffective.

Nowadays, the traditional style of lecture, in which an "expert" standing in front of a group presents information formally, is generally discouraged. Audiences are more sophisticated and expect more from seminars and presentations. Keep in mind that the seminar business is large and very competitive, and people are used to being informed in an interesting and entertaining way.

The potential problems with the lecture method include:

(a) It is passive; communication is one way. The low level of interaction tends to decrease learning levels.

(b) Many people are not very skilled at concentrating and listening for a long period of time.

(c) It is inflexible; everyone is bound to the pace of the lecturer.

(d) The quality of the delivery of the lecturer is a key factor in determining the success of this method.

(e) Having to take notes cuts down concentration, comprehension, learning, and remembering.

(f) There is less opportunity for thinking and problem-solving.

(g) It is not at all suitable for teaching physical skills.

However, if lectures are delivered well, there can be some positive points. Information can be transmitted at one time to a large group and in a standardized format. The lecturer can act as an example or a model of appropriate attitudes and ways of thinking. The lecturer can collect information from various sources and condense it into one good talk or lecture and tailor it directly to the needs of the group. A good lecture can work very well for highly motivated people.

If you are faced with having to present a formal lecture, here are some pointers:

(a) It's best to start by giving the objectives of your presentation and then explain exactly what you will cover and how you will present it.

(b) Pare your talk down to what is absolutely essential for the group; do not try to do too much. It is always better to do a small amount really well than overwhelm your audience with too much.

(c) Organize your talk so that you can summarize the main points as you go along.

(d) Increase your audience's interest, attention, motivation, understanding, and memory by building variety into your presentation. Use appropriate audiovisual aids, humor, anecdotes, gestures, and movement.

(e) Speak clearly and loudly enough so that everyone can hear you; use a microphone if needed. Do not speak too rapidly or too slowly; pause when necessary, but not for too long. Try to sound conversational and natural, enthusiastic and interested.

(f) Do not read from your notes. Refer to them occasionally, but look at people as you speak. In this way, you can measure interest levels and comprehension.

(g) Try as much as possible to involve the audience. You can do this by posing questions or problems at the beginning, asking them questions as you go along, inviting their questions and comments, holding a question and answer session at the end or at other points, or breaking the group into "buzz groups."

Sample #11 shows how you might organize your thoughts to plan your lecture.

b. ANALOGIES, ANECDOTES, AND OTHER VERBAL ILLUSTRATIONS

Language can help illustrate your point just as visual aids allow people to literally see what you are talking about. People understand and remember more easily if you can draw them a picture in words. We even say "I see" when something becomes clear to us or we can visualize what someone is talking about. Using analogies, frames of reference, anecdotes, and examples can help make your speech or presentation more interesting and can also help reinforce your themes.

1. Analogies

An analogy is the comparison of one thing to another, emphasizing the similarities (which outweigh their differences), so that listeners can compare the known to the unknown and apply previous knowledge to a new situation. For instance, if you're teaching people how to use a computer, you could suggest that a "directory" is like a drawer in a filing cabinet. When they look in the directory, they can see that there are various files displayed. By opening a file, they can then look anywhere inside as if it were really on their desk, and add to it or make changes. "Storing" is then like closing a file and putting it back in the drawer when they have finished.

Analogies are particularly useful when you are introducing new ideas or technical information that may seem abstract to your audience. Try to make an analogy to something concrete or familiar to most of the participants.

2. Frames of reference

A frame of reference is the existing set of attitudes, point of view, or knowledge which individuals bring to a new experience. In learning something new, individuals must build upon their existing frame of reference to master new knowledge. You can help them do this by presenting the new information in terms of learners' previous experiences. An introduction to a talk is a good place to use frames of reference.

For example, if you were trying to improve customer service in an organization, you could start by having the group

Topic: Retirement Planning

Purpose (what you want to achieve): Those attending will be able to choose appropriate retirement programs for selves.

Key points:

1. Importance of retirement planning and when to start

2. Deciding individual retirement needs in $.
   Various retirement vehicles to save in now.

3. Income Tax Planning

4. Will and Estate Planning

Aids to use and when (e.g., slides, overhead transparencies):

- slides on each subject area

- flip chart to write on as go along

- booklets on each retirement program

Introduction:
   Everyone retires, need to plan ahead;
      the earlier the better

Bridge:
   Agenda - what talk will cover and why
            - opportunity for questions

Main body: Go through each key point.
             Answer questions as go along.
             Use slides

Conclusion: - Summarize key points
             - Hand out booklets

Questions and answers:

         - Let participants ask about anything
       they want more information on, missed
       hearing about

Feedback/evaluation:

       Question and answer session should reflect
       group's interest.

consider what they want when they themselves are customers. They could give examples of good and bad service they have personally experienced. You can then move from their experiences and preferences to the more general issues affecting their own organization and its customers.

There are times when you want people to switch to another frame of reference so that they can analyze situations from another point of view to enhance their awareness and understanding. For example, in a presentation about developing sales skills, you might introduce a role play in which a salesperson has to take the role of a dissatisfied customer or a store manager. Discussions also offer a basic way for participants to hear different points of view and consider issues from others' frames of reference.

3. Anecdotes

Anecdotes are interesting and often amusing short stories, true or fictional, which are designed to illustrate a point. They must be appropriate to the specific audience to be meaningful and useful.

I have often used this anecdote when I have wanted to illustrate the importance of dressing appropriately for the occasion and how important making a first impression is. My husband used to recruit on a university campus. On one occasion, after interviewing several prospective graduates, he went to the washroom. There he saw a young man whom he had just interviewed undressing and giving his smart navy suit to another young man of similar build! My husband pretended not to notice what was happening and then pretended not to recognize the now smartly dressed second student when he came in to be interviewed. He was impressed with their resourcefulness and never did find out who actually owned the suit!

Your anecdote should provide enough colorful detail to bring the story alive for your listeners but not so much that they lose the point of the story or fall asleep waiting for the punch line. In the story above, for example, the detail of the *navy* suit allows the listener to visualize the amusing contrast between the conservative sobriety of the suit and the very unconservative idea of sharing a suit for interviews. However, if I began to describe the room in which the interviews were taking place, that would likely drag my audience away from the central point. Always keep in mind that you are telling the anecdote for a reason, not merely to be witty.

4. Examples

Use realistic examples to illustrate a principle, idea, or situation whenever possible; it's a natural way to engage interest. Be sure to choose appropriate examples from the group's frame of reference. If you draw on personal experience, choose examples that give practical illustrations and don't merely make you look important.

Practitioners in a field of work who are training their peers are often in a very good position to use examples from personal experience. For example, a human resources consultant was helping a group develop interviewing skills. She explained how silence could be used in a positive way, especially if combined with a smile or nod, to encourage the interviewee to continue talking or to give more information. One of the group asked if silence could be negative, too, and the consultant agreed, and gave a good example. Previously she was a volunteer at a women's shelter. One of the residents said that she had finally left her unhappy marriage and one of the reasons was that her husband had neither talked nor really listened to her for over 20 years! Silence was definitely a punishment in that case.

This kind of example can make a talk or discussion come alive. However, beware of overdoing personal examples to the point where they sound like you are blowing your own horn. I know a successful real estate broker who often gives real estate courses; he is able to give very good examples because of his day-to-day work. However, students on his programs have confided that they do not appreciate the way he gives these realistic examples because they seem more intended to impress the students than to help them learn.

If you find that you do have many examples from personal experience that would be helpful to your seminar, but you are afraid that using them would sound self-serving, you might describe them as happening to "another trainer your know," or "a colleague of yours," etc.

5. Use verbal illustrations carefully

Before using any illustrations, ask yourself the following:

(a) Does it relate directly to the point? Make sure it contributes to getting your message across.

(b) Is it accurate?

(c) Is it clear? Use enough detail for clarity, but do not bore or confuse them with too much.

(d) Is this the best way to present the information?

(e) Is it appropriate to this audience? It must fit their experience, interest, and ability level.

c. LIGHTS, CAMERA, ACTION! — YOUR ROLE AS "DIRECTOR"

Often, the learning process has been compared to a theatrical event where the presenter has the role of the leading actor — the star in the spotlight — and the learners are the audience, watching and listening to the performance. This style stresses one-way communication, with success depending largely on the performing ability of the presenter.

It is far better to cast yourself, the facilitator, as the "director" of this "production." Directors, in films and theater, have a clear concept of the outcome they want, and they endeavor to draw out the best from the cast and technicians to achieve those results.

Think of yourself as a director: you need to have your objectives clearly defined, determine how you will achieve them, and use the participants to get the results you want. Thus, they are more like actors than audience members.

d. GET THEM INVOLVED

Many times it is effective to involve participants directly in learning activities. This is particularly helpful if you are running a workshop or smaller seminar. Interactive learning involves group members in specially designed activities and enhances their learning in the process. The term *facilitator* is often used these days, pointing to the changing role of trainers. The emphasis now is less on being the "expert" who stands at the front and informs and instructs the group, than on the facilitator who enables others to understand and learn better by involving them in activities drawing on their capacities, experience, skills, knowledge, and potential.

Interactive techniques —

(a) offer variety, increasing motivation, interest, and attention;

(b) stimulate thinking, reasoning, and reflecting;

(c) improve understanding, learning, and memory;

(d) encourage participants to practice specific skills that need to be improved and developed; and

(e) help develop teamwork, interpersonal communication, and insight into group dynamics and individual differences.

Some interactive techniques can be used on large groups as well, but you must plan carefully and practice your control of the process so you feel comfortable and it works well. Techniques such as role playing are less appropriate in larger groups, but questioning, discussions, and case studies can all work well. It works even better if you can wander around and talk to some of the smaller groups as they are working together. This helps minimize the feeling of distance that can occur when you deal with larger numbers of people. When breaking a large group into small groups, give clear instructions as to what you want them to do and for how long, and ensure you stick to the time. I have sometimes even used a bell or small whistle to regain a group's attention and get them to stop talking!

Whatever technique you use, you must always point out first what is to happen and why, what the ground rules are, what their tasks are, what they must accomplish, and how long they have to do it.

e. ASKING QUESTIONS

When used well, questioning techniques can be very effective in gaining and maintaining interest, prompting thinking and reasoning, and improving understanding, learning, and memory. You can also show respect for the group's intelligence, ideas, and experiences by asking for and rewarding their contributions.

When you ask a question, always make sure it is clear and concise. If the reaction to one of your questions is a blank look, perhaps you should think again and rephrase your question.

Put only one question at a time, unless you can easily enumerate what you are asking and still be clear and concise. Give time for your audience to think and respond. Many speakers feel uncomfortable with silence and often jump in too quickly with a comment or even the answer if their audience's silence seems prolonged. This can frustrate those who are thinking, or give others a way out, since they will quickly realize that all they need to do is keep quiet and you will go to someone else or do all the work and give the answer yourself! You can always say: "It's okay. Take your time, think about it before you answer," or smile and nod to show that you will be patient and wait for a response.

When you get an answer, even if it is wrong, your first reaction should be to reward the answerer. If you get a wrong answer, do not immediately respond with "No." Instead, reward the attempt; for example, say "Good try, but not quite what I was looking for." Then help the individual get the right answer by giving hints and clues. You want to encourage individuals to contribute, whether they are right or not, and help them to learn effectively.

Generally, there are three types of questions that are effective in presentations:

(a) Overheads

(b) Direct questions to an individual

(c) Probes

1. Overhead questions

An overhead is a general question directed to the whole group. When using this type of question, wait for a volunteer to answer. This way everyone has a chance to think about your question and the opportunity to respond. You will sound confident that someone will answer if you start your question with: "Who can tell me..." rather than: "Can anyone tell me...."

2. Direct questions

A direct question to an individual is best used when you want to single someone out because you know he or she has specific experience or knowledge you want to draw on. Make sure you do this in a non-threatening way. You can say, for example: "If I may ask you to share your experience with us, Chris," and then ask the question.

If you are not after specific information from a particular person, the best way to ask a direct question is by asking your question first, pausing, then tagging the person's name on the end. For example, you might ask, "What would make you decide that your car battery is dead...Chris?"

In this way, you give everyone time to think of the answer (and hope they all do), before directing the question to one person. If you start the question with a specific person's name: "Chris, can you tell us..." you are giving everyone else permission to switch off their thinking processes and you could also be putting Chris on the spot.

Of course, you should never put a question to someone who you are fairly sure does not know the answer, particularly if you are tempted to do this to get that person to pay attention, wake up, or stop talking to someone else! Even if the others understand your reason, they will not really respect you for doing it. Your technique may work in the short term, but you will probably alienate at least the person you singled out, and you may be the victim of revenge at a later date!

3. Probes

Probes are questions that can be overhead or directed to an individual. What makes probes different is that they are questions that follow on from the response you get to your initial question. I have already mentioned that if you get a wrong answer, or no answer, you might try giving hints or clues in a follow-up question or statement to help the individual come up with the right answer. An initial question followed by a probe might go like this:

You: "What is the new legislation a supervisor must deal with in safety meetings — John?"

John: Silence.

You: "Okay, the initials are W.H.I.M.I.S."

John: "Of course — Workplace Hazardous Materials Information System."

You: "Right!"

4. Using questions to encourage learning

Whenever you ask a question, you want to try to get the most out of your participants. Whether you use overhead, direct, or probing questions, avoid a closed-end question that will elicit a simple yes or no or a specific answer that doesn't encourage discussion. For example:

Question: "What would you put on a sprained ankle to stop it swelling?"

Answer: "An ice pack."

In contrast, open-ended questions are far less direct. A clear-cut answer isn't possible and the person responding can expand and give more information and ideas. For example:

Question: "What do you think about involving employees in decision making?"

This question forces the respondent to make a judgment and answer with thought. It may also stimulate discussion among the group. You might get an answer such as "It depends on what the decision is about — whether it is something that really affects employees so it would matter that they are involved." Then you might say, "Right. Can you give me an example of when it would matter to them?" This can start a useful dialogue.

f. PROBLEM-SOLVING EXERCISES

Problem-solving activities can be used to develop specific principles as well as to teach general ones. Exercises can be tailored to meet the needs of participants, especially if you use names, places, or situations with which they can easily identify or which they can relate their own work experience.

A colleague of mine who is a computer programming instructor often puts up "A Friendly Quiz" on the overhead projector. The quiz contains realistic problem situations

49

that he asks participants to solve in a reasonable time. He then goes through the quiz, asking for answers and offering to explain any points that have caused difficulties. This way he makes sure everything is clear before moving on, the participants get good practice, and it gives them immediate feedback on how they are doing.

When training supervisors, I make up appropriate situations. For example, I invent employees with common performance problems that they then have to discuss in small groups so they can suggest solutions. I also often devise "in-basket" exercises where participants are given a list or collection of items that should reflect what they might typically find in their own in-baskets — memos, notes, mail, messages, and other tasks they have to handle. Individually or in small groups, they have to determine the priority to assign to each item and what action to take, when and why, including what to delegate.

Participants usually like problem-solving exercises and they learn much more easily by using them.

g. DISCUSSIONS

Discussions must be purposeful and focused; you must decide the reason for a discussion and what you want to achieve. This is not a technique that is appropriate for the transmission of facts or new material or for use with inarticulate individuals who have little experience or knowledge to discuss.

Most adults will be open to small group discussions if they are well primed on the purpose and how to organize their discussion group. For total group discussions, participants have to feel comfortable with you and each other so they are open to expressing their ideas and opinions in front of others. You will need to control the dominant talkers and encourage the quieter ones to participate. You may need to practice skills for leading discussions, for example,

listening, encouraging, paraphrasing, stimulating, and orchestrating discussions. It is also useful to develop skills in group dynamics, including conflict management.

Ample time and space is needed for this method, but well-run discussions have several advantages:

(a) Motivation and interest is increased because of variety and active involvement.

(b) Participants feel their ideas are valued and that they have something to contribute.

(c) Small group discussions are good for testing and comparing knowledge and ideas. Individuals have the chance to analyze and deal with problems, exchange ideas and consider others' views.

(d) Discussions provide the opportunity to work in a small group to reach a common goal, which can be important in the real work setting.

(e) Participants can gain experience in presenting ideas, listening, and appropriate interpersonal and group behavior.

(f) An opportunity is provided for exploring professional values and attitudes.

(g) When there is discussion after a presentation or as you go along you can evaluate how well individuals have understood the material and how they interpret particular factors. This may lead you to take appropriate corrective measures when necessary.

Remember that a discussion must stay focused and it must be directed by you — the leader. Participants will become bored and frustrated if they feel the discussion is "going in circles." Here are some pointers for effectively leading a discussion in a small group:

(a) Determine your objectives ahead of time. Decide what you want the participants to do and how long they will need to do it.

(b) Write down instructions, then give these clearly at the start so that everyone is well prepared and can be properly organized.

(c) Structure the groups to suit the purpose. Let participants choose their own group or you choose. There should be a cross section of roles, responsibilities, and experience in each group and a balance of personalities.

(d) Avoid having a dominant person in the same group as a less talkative individual. For maximum participation of all group members, limit the group size to five.

(e) Organize the discussion so that there are definite steps. Each group can be assigned the same or different tasks. Then have each group report back on their discussion and the answers or solutions they have arrived at.

(f) Let participants know when their time is nearly up so they can complete their allotted task. Allow time for each group to report on its major points, perhaps write these up, and add any important points which did not surface from the discussions.

(g) Summarize the discussion for everyone at the end as a way of concluding. Add any key points that you may have wanted to surface but that did not.

When running discussions with larger numbers, you really need to set guidelines and stick to them. For example, set a time limit, announce when time is almost up, then enforce the ending. Call for silence when you want the groups to listen to each other and ask for feedback from specific groups one at a time.

You don't have to appear as a bully, "carrying a big stick," but you do have to stay in control, keep everyone on track, and allow sufficient time for each group. You can still smile and be pleasant, but demonstrate that you are holding the discussion to achieve a specific purpose.

h. CASE STUDIES

Case studies are prepared descriptions of realistic scenarios that may be based on actual events. Groups can discuss these scenarios together and devise their own solutions. You can ask participants to suggest the best course of action or answer some questions.

When I was conducting a workshop for supervisors on their role in training their staff, I made up a case about a company that changed some of its operations and then had problems with staff working under the new system. The participants had to analyze what was now going wrong and why, and how it might have been avoided. Each group had to answer these questions: What training will staff need to deal with the new situation? How could a training program be designed that would meet the needs of different staff members? After the groups had reported their answers, we tried to relate these issues to their own work situations.

Case studies can involve participants in realistic situations and stimulate consideration, analysis, and discussion of significant factors in a situation, as well as helping to develop judgment and decision-making and problem-solving skills.

They enable participants to analyze different viewpoints and test their solutions and/or ideas — all of which promotes learning.

When you use case studies, keep in mind the following:

(a) You can control the direction by giving as little or as much information as desired. Again, you must have a specific purpose for the activity and determine the end result desired.

(b) Direct the activity in terms of what and how it is conducted. Organize the participants in small groups to discuss a realistic situation; have them analyze it and perhaps come up with a solution.

(c) Each small group should report back and then all participants can compare and evaluate what each small group has done.

(d) Finally, get the group to summarize what has been discussed. Evaluate whether the objectives have been met.

A variation on the case study is the *incident process*. With this method, you present a brief summary of a situation, usually a real-life work situation, that is much shorter than a case study. I often get members of the group to contribute their own examples for analysis and discussion.

The small groups decide what information they have, what they need, and how to use it, which is more like the real job atmosphere. They can go off on tangents, too. The groups can ask questions, one at a time, and be given answers. You can record the answers and the number of questions each group asks, then analyze the questions and see which group gets the best results.

i. ROLE PLAYING

Another useful technique involves having participants act out situations using previously written roles which they are assigned. This is known as *role playing*. It can be used to help participants identify with others' points of view, attitudes, beliefs, feelings, and to practice interpersonal skills such as interviewing and sales techniques.

There are two procedures for role playing: single group and multiple. Which one you choose will depend on your objectives. In single-group role play, one group performs and everyone else watches. Then they all discuss what led to a particular outcome or effect. The role players can benefit from the comments of these observers, since they usually are less aware of what they did, how they did it, and the effect of their actions on others.

With multiple role play, you divide your workshop into small groups and all groups practice role play at the same time. This is my preferred technique because it gives more opportunity for practice and it minimizes self-consciousness. If the roles are the same for all groups, there might be differences in outcome that can then be discussed. Multiple role play is particularly effective for maximizing the opportunities for participants to practice new attitudes, behaviors, and skills.

Role play helps develop sensitivity to others' feelings and is best for intensive training, for advanced work with small groups, and for demonstrations. However, some people will be reluctant to be put under the spotlight. If you find participants are uncomfortable at the prospect, you could give them observer roles; however, do try some persuading and encouraging first.

Usually role playing is more successful after a program has been underway for a while, that is, when participants feel more comfortable with you and each other.

If you do want to conduct a role play, keep in mind that how you set the scene, select the players, and assign the roles is very important. First, explain the purpose of the exercise and then tell everyone the procedure that you will follow. You could write up the steps with a time allocation for each:

(a) Distribute background information for everyone to read: 5 minutes

(b) Workshop divides into role-playing groups (specify number, composition, choice)

(c) Assign (or let them choose) and distribute roles; everyone reads and digests: 10 minutes.

(d) Arrange the room; role playing starts and continues: 20 minutes

(e) Each group discusses outcome: 10 minutes

(f) Total workshop discussion, evaluation, and summary: 20 minutes

When roles are distributed, you will want to explain something about each role, but limit it to how much you can say without giving the game away. It's a good idea to assign roles to participants who need the practice. For example, if interviewing skills are to be developed through role playing, a participant who is less experienced in this area could volunteer to be the interviewer.

Instructions about how to perform the roles are also important. Encourage the participants to use their role-play information sheets as scripts. Usually, you will want them to read the information sheet to get the feel of the role and then put these aside during the actual role play. Always emphasize that they are not being tested on their acting ability!

Finally, it is useful for each group to have an observer who takes notes for later discussion. Make sure you instruct the observer to sit a little apart from the action so he or she does not disturb the "actors."

j. COMBINATIONS

Many of the above techniques can be combined. For instance, a case study can be combined with a discussion, or a problem-solving situation could be followed by role playing. You could also videotape a role play for discussion, evaluation, or illustration.

Your only limit is your imagination. If you keep your objectives in mind along with the needs of your audience, you can't go wrong!

5 *A picture is worth a thousand words: using audiovisuals*

Audiovisuals are anything that will help you provide illustrations as part of your session and appeal to different senses. The more senses an aid appeals to, the more effective the communication and learning will be. The most commonly used audiovisual aids are overhead projectors, slides, boards, films, videos, and handouts.

a. THE BENEFITS OF USING AUDIOVISUAL AIDS

Visual aids, from boards to flipcharts, audio- or videotapes to overhead projectors, are a good way to add variety to your presentation. Audiovisuals can be combined with other aspects of your presentation to increase motivation and learning.

Audiovisuals emphasize the importance of the senses in learning. We notice and learn most through our eyes, so we should involve sight as much as possible. The next most important sense is hearing. This sense is often overused, particularly in the form of listening to the instructor's voice. Once a sense is overused, it loses its effectiveness; an instructor should never be the one who does all the talking. That's why combining sight *and* hearing produces considerable impact. The other senses are less valuable, but may be more applicable for certain subjects like chemistry or when acquiring physical skills when smell and touch are appropriate.

Audiovisuals can simplify instruction by making clear what words alone may leave in doubt. It's much easier to show relationships between things when you can show that one thing is larger than another or show how complex something is by breaking it up into many parts.

Repetition is needed for learning and remembering. An aid can be used to repeat something in a slightly different way. Aids help people understand and remember better and for longer. They create and hold interest, provide variety, and emphasize what is especially important.

If you choose audiovisual aids to suit your purpose and use them well, your participants will benefit. Since people have different learning skills and learning styles, use a variety of methods to accommodate all trainees and the objectives they are to achieve.

b. OBJECTS AND MODELS

Whenever possible bring in the real thing. This gives everyone the chance to see what is being discussed. If you are showing off the benefits of a new computer program, have a computer set up with the program running. If you are running a first aid course, you might arrange for volunteers to act as "victims."

Models and exhibits look like the real thing, but are either larger or smaller and therefore more useful. They may be schematic representations and thus, show parts of the real thing in more detail. Models can be simple and easy to make and do not have to be expensive.

c. PRINTED MATERIALS

Printed materials can include work documents such as forms, prepared reference materials such as books and manuals, or handout materials such as summaries, notes, diagrams, or outlines to complete. These can improve concentration and participation during the session since they save individuals having to take too many notes as well as ensuring that they have what is needed for reference and review.

Consider how and when you wish to distribute handouts. If you give them out before the session, participants may be overwhelmed by the volume or they may read them and be confused by some of the information.

If you do want materials read ahead of time, be sure to give clear instructions in your pre-seminar package. At the start of your session, check that participants have done the reading and then, before going on, discuss or clarify any misunderstandings.

Handouts can be a source of distraction; for that reason, I prefer to give out materials only at the point when I want them to be looked at. If the material is for later reading, I advise participants of this and ask them to put the handouts aside. However you choose to distribute handouts, tell participants that they will be available — either as the seminar progresses or afterwards. If you don't, you may find that participants are scrambling to take notes while you speak — only to find out later that their efforts were wasted because you had handouts prepared for later distribution!

If any of your handouts are excerpts from previously published material, be sure you get proper permission and copyright clearance before using them.

d. BOARDS AND FLIPCHARTS

Boards and flipcharts are generally available and fairly simple to use. Plan ahead how you want to use the board. Keep it simple, make it orderly, and do not overcrowd the board.

Whiteboards are quite versatile because slides or overhead transparencies can be projected onto them. You can combine projected materials with your own notes on the board.

On magnetic boards, you can display charts or diagrams held by magnets. You can also put magnetic strips to the back of pictures, models etc., and arrange these on the board. This is most effective medium for creating a gradual buildup of information or for showing alternate arrangements. Most chalkboards are magnetic.

Flipcharts should only be used for a small audience because of their limited visibility. You can have prepared pages or write on the chart during your session. They can be useful during meetings when you want to tear off the pages to display what has been written up or to use later to produce minutes or action plans.

Keep these pointers in mind when using boards and flipcharts:

(a) Print — don't write. Most people's printing is clearer than their writing.

(b) Print large enough so everyone in the room can read the board. Test readability by walking around the room to see how legible your words are from all angles and which colors show up best.

(c) Use point form when writing on a board. Full sentences fill your board with unnecessary information, making it harder to pick out the essential information. Points, key words, or phrases are much better and guide your audience about what to take down for their own notes. Erase what is not really needed so it is not distracting.

(d) Use colored markers or pens, underlining, and capital letters to add emphasis.

(e) Don't obstruct the board while you are printing. Do not talk into the board: it is better to speak first then write (or draw), or write first and then turn and speak to the group again.

(f) Remember that most whiteboards have shiny surfaces, so try to cut down glare from lights or windows.

(g) When using flipcharts, prevent them becoming a distraction by turning over the page when you want the group to stop looking at it.

e. PREPARED CHARTS AND DIAGRAMS

Any charts and diagrams you use should be clear, simple, and easily seen by everyone and should be introduced when appropriate in the session. For example, when conducting orientation sessions to new employees, it is often helpful to show an organization chart of the company so that you can clearly explain how different departments are interconnected, how each reports to another, etc.

f. RECORDINGS

Although sound is less effective than sight for learning, audio aids can be useful. They provide variety, particularly if they have one or more different speakers.

Some time ago, when I was conducting a course on assertiveness, I used an audiotape that I had made of a short radio interview with the author Wayne Dyer, who had just written a book on the topic. It provided another insight into the topic, and I recommended his book, too.

Audio material must be clearly audible and must not last too long; attention spans are short! Be very careful to minimize the rather passive nature of this aid: introduce it well and involve participants. For example, you might ask questions that can only be answered by listening to the tape. Or you might tell them what to listen for and have a discussion afterwards.

Some copyright protection extends to use of recorded materials. Be aware of copyright law when choosing and using sound recordings. For more on copyright, see section **k.** below.

g. OVERHEADS, FILM, AND SLIDES

1. The overhead projector

The overhead projector has a flat glass surface on which you place a transparency that is projected onto a large screen. You can purchase blank, clear or colored transparencies at most stores where office supplies are sold. These can be used for permanent printing or for writing on with special overhead projector pens. Prepared overhead transparencies (OHTs) save time and can be used over and over again.

Alternatively, you can use blank transparencies, writing on them during the lesson instead of using a flipchart or board. I often put a blank transparency on top of a prepared one and write on that, which can then be washed and re-used. This way you don't mark the permanent one and it can be used again.

There are several advantages to using an overhead projector in a presentation. This medium works well with all sizes of groups because you can control the size of the image. If you need a larger image, you simply move the projector further from the screen. No special lighting is necessary, and you can maintain eye contact with the group while using it because you are looking at the transparency while the participants look at the screen. The projector can be easily switched off when you want to regain attention or you no longer want the group focusing on the projected material. I often put "post-it" notes on transparencies with notes or reminders to myself, then I peel these off before using them, and stick them on again afterwards. You can also write notes on the frame or paper.

Different techniques can be used to great effect. You can reveal a small amount of an image at a time by covering what you do not wish to show with a sheet of paper, then later exposing the next part. You can also add to information by overlaying individual transparencies. Sample #12 shows three overhead transparencies that combine to show a new processing system.

Here are some hints for using overhead projectors effectively:

(a) Set up the machine and screen for optimum visibility: it is often better at an angle to the group (say, across a corner) rather than straight on, right at the front.

(b) Switch it off when you want to control or direct attention.

(c) Always check that the picture is correctly projected onto the screen (not off on a wall, or on the ceiling!) and is in focus.

(d) DO NOT look at the screen onto which the image is projected. Use a pencil or pointer on the OHT to point to specific details. This way you can maintain eye contact with your audience and avoid obstructing vision with your body.

(e) Stand on the left of the machine if you are right-handed (and vice versa), especially when pointing to or writing on OHTs.

(f) Take the time to ensure that you place the OHT on the screen straight. It's frustrating for participants to have to look at a crooked image.

(g) Keep OHTs simple and limit the color you use. If you have a lot of detail, expose the information gradually. Use a sheet of paper to uncover one point at a time rather than the whole OHT at once. (See section **i.** below for guidelines on lettering visibility and size related to viewing distance from the screen.)

(h) Do not move the machine while it is switched on since this can damage the expensive lamp inside.

(i) If you will be handing out print copies of your overheads, let your participants know so they don't waste time taking notes and can give you their full attention.

2. Slides

Slides are made using slide film instead of negative film. They can then be projected through a projector onto a screen.

Slides have quite a few advantages. They are good for use with small groups, and even for very large groups if you have a large screen. For formal, one-way presentations, slides are also effective. If they are well photographed, they give a dramatic and professional effect. You can make slides yourself, so you can be selective as to what you show. Your pictures can be authentic, up-to-date, and easily updated.

Slide presentations work well with other methods of delivery — questions and discussion for example. You can change the order, vary the rate of delivery or show just a few at a time, and combine them with audiotapes for additional benefits.

When using slides:

(a) Number the slides in the tray so you can make up notes for yourself referring to the slide numbers. You can also sort them more easily if they fall out!

(b) Keep your slides relevant and simple, with a limited amount of words on each. Ensure that they are visible and in focus.

(c) Use a remote control device and special light pointer, if necessary, and stand to the side of the screen so you do not block vision. Give explanations where they are needed and relate to the topic.

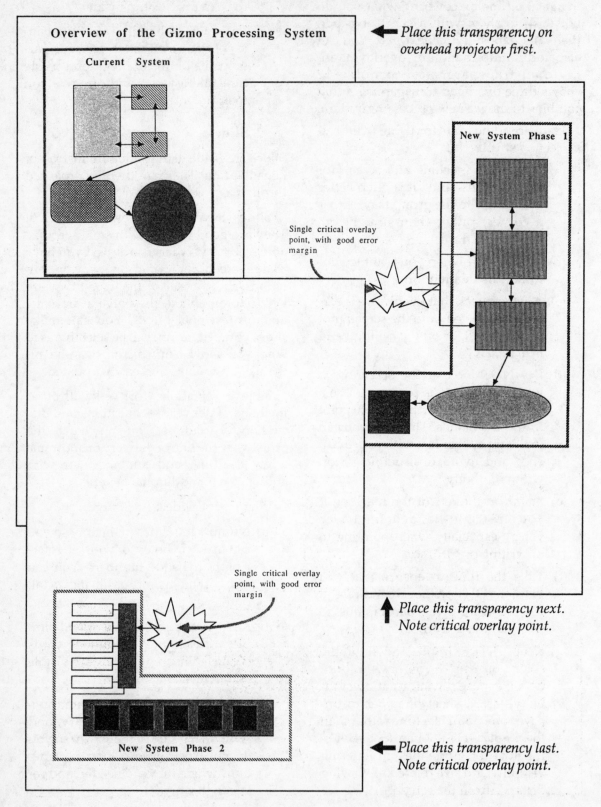

Overview of the Gizmo Processing System

Place this transparency on overhead projector first.

Current System

New System Phase 1

Single critical overlay point, with good error margin

Place this transparency next. Note critical overlay point.

Single critical overlay point, with good error margin

New System Phase 2

Place this transparency last. Note critical overlay point.

58

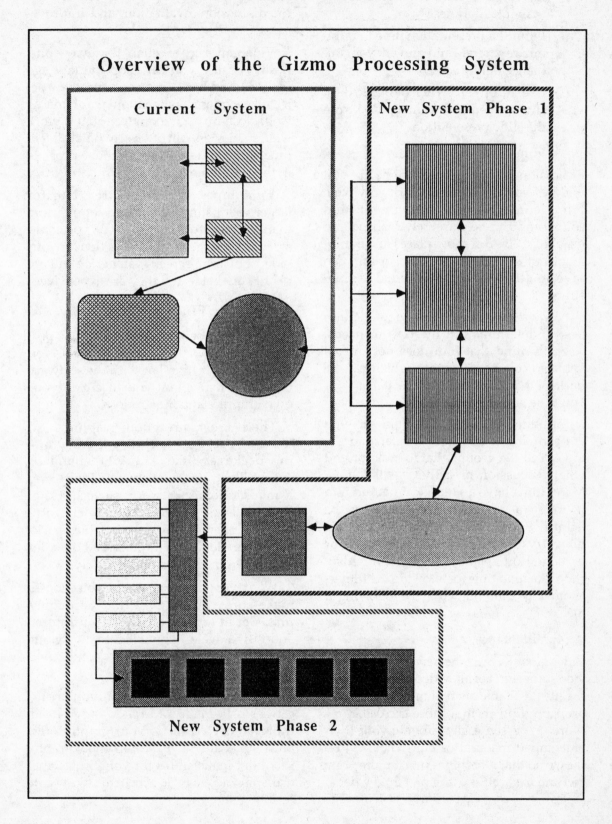

Overview of the Gizmo Processing System

Current System

New System Phase 1

New System Phase 2

(d) Since the room has to be darkened, try to have dimmed lights rather than total darkness.

(e) Limit the presentation time to minimize eye strain and prevent your audience falling asleep.

(f) Use the on/off switch or blank, dark slides when you want a pause from the slide presentation.

3. Films

Professionally made 16mm films are still widely available and can work very well. Films combine sight, movement, and sound and can be extremely realistic and dramatic. You can show places and equipment not otherwise available. A film can save you time by showing edited demonstrations.

Always make sure you review the film first to determine if it meets your needs. Keep in mind that film does not suit all venues. You need a room which can be darkened well, which makes it hard for you to see reactions.

Introduce the film and explain why you are showing it and how it relates to the topic. Tell the group what to look for and what discussion or activity will follow. Many films have a great deal packed into them, so a summary at the end can be helpful. Since film is rather a passive medium, try to build in other activities in your presentation relating to the film. Also, choose a good time for showing the film — avoid any time immediately following a meal.

4. Videotapes

Videotapes have all the benefits of film and then some. First of all, videotapes are more readily available than film and you will probably find them a more accessible resource. You can easily provide your own videotaped material or edit what will be shown so that it becomes much more your own aid. As well as using prepared videos, you can videotape participants practicing skills, so the recordings can be shown later for discussion, evaluation, and improvement.

Videotapes are excellent for review purposes because you can stop the tape, go forward and back, and concentrate on selected segments when you want to. As well, close-up and zoom techniques work well, so viewers can often see something in much greater detail than might be possible in the classroom or the field.

Videotapes are not appropriate for larger groups unless you can set up more than one monitor. Alternatively, you could arrange for large-screen projection for your video, but large-screen systems are still not readily available and they are expensive.

h. COMPUTER GRAPHICS

If you have a personal computer and produce your own handout materials, you may already be familiar with the software programs that allow you to create your own graphics and illustrations.

There are many good graphics and drawing packages to choose from. Drawing packages, like Aldus Freehand or Adobe Illustrator, allow you to draw using a mouse. Some software, such as Corel Draw, allows you to access a "clip art" library of generic images. Graphics packages, like Harvard Graphics or Lotus, let you create charts and graphs easily.

Whatever graphics package you choose, make sure you check it out thoroughly first. Get in touch with the manufacturer and visit a dealer who will let you try out the program. Make sure it is compatible with your existing system.

Any graphic or illustration you create can easily be made into a slide or overhead transparency. Transfer your graphics file onto a disk and have a commercial graphics outlet make slides for you. Slides and transparencies produced this way can have high resolution and a wide choice of colors.

As well as enhancing handout materials, computer graphics can be run as a program and shown on a monitor or projected onto a high-resolution screen. This lets you demonstrate a simulated result. For example, you can manipulate figures in a spreadsheet and instantly show your audience how the end result is changed. This kind of interactive use of computer graphics is essential for presentations that involve computer-assisted instruction and computer-assisted learning.

With computer graphics programs, it is possible to create a complete electronic presentation. Dissolves and transitions can be created on computer, similar to using two or more slide projectors. You can also use other kinds of transitions like dissolves and wipes.

With computer animation programs, you can animate your computer images and add sound. You can also scan illustrations and photographs and create computer images or slides. **Note:** if you use a scanner, be cautious about using published materials because these are protected by copyright.

Interactive computer-assisted presentations are more common in business settings, perhaps with a small group of learners. As with other audiovisual techniques, consider your audience's needs and the demands of your subject.

Though convenient and professional looking, computer graphics do have their limits. Use your design sense and find the right balance that will enhance the look of your materials and help your audience learn. No matter how brilliant the images or clever the computer tricks, don't leave your audience staring at a computer screen for long periods. Boredom and "video burnout" are likely, so the rules about varying your presentation still apply.

i. MAXIMIZING THE USE OF AUDIOVISUAL AIDS

A good aid is unified and easy to understand. It makes just one main point; there is nothing irrelevant to the learning or the issue. Avoid films, videotapes, and audio recordings that use cryptic phrases, jargon, and abbreviations, unless you are absolutely sure your audience is familiar with these terms. The message should be told in the fewest possible words, symbols, or pictures. Too much detail forces your audience to choose whether to pay attention to you or to your visual.

Decide on the main point you want your audience to get, then omit whatever does not directly support it, but not at the expense of comprehension, of course. Reduce the text to essentials, use brief phrases; break the text down into bullet points where appropriate. Build up from the simple or the general to the complex.

A good aid must be accurate. There should be no unexplained distortions, no facts missing, and no wrong facts — and definitely no typos or grammatical errors.

Good aids are visible and legible. Lettering should be large and bold. Use a strong, readable typeface. Spidery, thin fonts are hard to read and frustrating. Color can be used to help visibility, but keep these points in mind:

(a) Use restraint in the number of colors used in each aid. Keep consistent any symbolism of colors (if a specific color is used to represent something meaningful).

(b) Lighter tones (tints or pastels) should be used for the background.

(c) Different colors have different psychological impacts: red is warm and stimulating; blue is cool and calming, but may have depressing effects; yellow is warm, capricious, with sunny overtones; green is pleasant and healthy; orange is stimulating; purple gives messages of dignity and reserve.

(d) Colors are also related to visibility. Warm colors (red, orange, yellow) appear larger than cool ones. A light color appears brighter against a black background than a white one. Strongly saturated colors seem to have more weight than pastels. The best color combinations for visibility, from best to worst, are :

- Black on yellow
- Black on orange
- Orange on navy blue
- Green on white
- Red on white
- Black on white
- Navy blue on white
- White on navy blue
- Orange on black
- White on black
- White on green
- White on red
- White on purple
- Purple on white
- Navy blue on yellow
- Navy blue on blue
- Purple on yellow

When choosing sizes for your lettering, consider these guidelines on visibility and legibility based on the viewing distance.

8'	¼"
16'	½"
32'	1"
64'	2"

j. A STITCH IN TIME...

As discussed, visual aids can add immensely to the effectiveness of your session, but they can also turn it into a horror show if you are not well prepared. Think what would happen if 30 minutes of your 2-hour session focused on a slide presentation and the bulb burned out as you turned the projector on?

Here are some things you should do to prevent any audiovisual disasters:

- Arrive early so you can check the setup and test any equipment and aids you plan to use.
- Check that screens and flipcharts are visible and that distracting light isn't reflecting on them.
- Test videotape machines, slide projectors, overheads, etc.
- Have available spare lamps for projectors.
- Check for all light switches so you can easily turn them on and off and make sure blinds and curtains are easily opened and closed.
- Plan a space to put your transparencies, notes, and other requirements.

1. Your professional kit

It is quite helpful to prepare a permanent kit to keep all your notes, transparencies, etc. organized and ready to use whenever you need them. Consider including the following items:

(a) Blank transparencies for overhead projectors and water-soluble projector pens in two or three colors,

(b) Magic markers for flip-chart

(c) Dry markers for white boards

(d) Chalk, if using a chalkboard (a chalk holder is very useful)

(e) A few paper towels and tissues (good for cleaning white boards and overhead projectors, as well as for mopping up spills.

(f) Extension cord (unless you are certain you will not need one or it will be provided)

(g) Extendible pointer

(h) Masking tape, thumb tacks, magnets (if using flipcharts or your own charts or diagrams)

2. Survival skills

If you are using any form of audiovisual equipment, it is well worth your learning some basic maintenance skills. Apart from ensuring that your presentation runs smoothly, it will also reduce your stress level if you do not have to worry about what might go wrong.

Make sure you can at least change defective lamps in projectors (always check that a spare one is available), un-jam slides, and, perhaps, diagnose other faults that others can then fix for you.

Wherever you are, find out who is available if you need help (especially with equipment), and how to get hold of someone in a hurry. Meet the person in charge of maintenance and audiovisual equipment beforehand, if possible, since people are usually more helpful if there is some personal relationship already established.

k. COPYRIGHT

It is illegal and unprofessional to use without permission any materials that have been produced by someone else. These include instructional aids such as handouts, overhead transparencies, slides, cartoons, pictures, written materials, case studies, role plays, and other exercises written by someone else, and recorded material such as video- and audiotapes.

Copyright law can trip you up in unexpected ways. For example, while the audio *recording* of material is not copyrighted, the *text* itself *is*, whether in printed or recorded form. So, if you wanted to play a lengthy passage from a tape about motivating employees, you would need permission from whoever owns the copyright in the tape's script.

Don't take any chances on copyright violation. When in doubt — leave it out!

Many books and manuals contain articles or learning activities that the authors invite trainers to reproduce and use, provided that the source is acknowledged. When I was producing a students' manual to accompany a "telecollege" course, I wanted to reproduce a cartoon I had seen in a newspaper. The cartoonist kindly gave his permission for its use when I wrote to him explaining why I wanted to reprint it. So if you know the source, you can ask for permission to incorporate others' material into your program.

In Canada, for more information about copyright, you can contact —

Department of Consumer and Corporate Affairs, Canada
Place du Portage, Phase 1
Ottawa/Hull, Quebec
K1A 0C9

In the United States, you can contact —

Copyright Office
LM 455
Library of Congress
Washington, D.C.
20559

Use Checklist #1 to help you plan your presentation whenever you are using audiovisuals.

CHECKLIST #1
USING AUDIOVISUALS

☐ Have I chosen the right visuals for the subject, the audience, and the room?

☐ Have I underestimated the intelligence of my audience by using "tiny tot" visuals? Am I using my visuals merely as a cue card for myself? (If so, get rid of them. Use key word notes for yourself.)

☐ Have I considered the cost and time my visuals will take to make? Do have the funds and the time needed to allow for preparation and rehearsal?

☐ Have I simplified my ideas so they can be demonstrated clearly?

☐ Do my visuals clarify or merely support? (If the latter, don't use them.)

☐ Do my visuals have a consistent basic structure and unity?

☐ Have I put too much material on one visual? (One idea per visual is the rule.)

☐ Is there anything on the visual that is not pertinent to the point being presented?

☐ Does the eye go to the most important concept on the visual through choice of color, typeface, and line or does the eye jump around because of false signals?

☐ Are my visuals free from complicating typefaces, art techniques, and symbols?

☐ Can my audience easily grasp what they see? Are my visuals direct and to the point?

☐ Do my visuals give pertinent information without distortion?

☐ Can my visuals be seen from any point in the audience? Are they aligned properly?

☐ Have I planned two to four rehearsals with my visuals before I make my presentation?

☐ Is the equipment available for the day of my presentation?

☐ Have I made a solid booking for the equipment I'll need?

6 It's showtime!

You may well have a wealth of knowledge and skills to pass on to others, but if your personal style puts your audience to sleep, no one is going to benefit from your wisdom. You need a little "show business" to make your presentation interesting and, yes, entertaining. This chapter focuses on how to gain others' attention and keep it so they will get the most out of the session.

a. HOW WE COMMUNICATE

When you think about making a presentation, you probably think mostly about "public speaking" and the importance of words and language. But when people communicate face-to-face, 93% of the impact comes from the non-verbal aspects of communication. You may not even be aware of how you communicate non-verbally through your gestures, facial expressions, appearance, etc., but these factors will send some of the first messages to your audience and must be considered in your complete "package."

Basically we use a combination of nine communication systems to get a message across:

- Words
- Eye contact
- Facial expressions
- Tone of voice
- Body movement
- Gestures
- Appearance (including artifacts)
- Proxemics (i.e., the distance between a speaker and the audience)
- Smell

Most often we use words plus other physical, nonverbal cues. The nonverbal systems can add to what is said or belie it. If the nonverbals give the same message as the words, you convey sincerity and credibility.

The two most important nonverbals are eye contact, which makes listeners feel you are interested in them, and facial expression, which shows how you feel about what you are saying and about the audience. Your tone of voice is a close third runner-up. Usually, voice is more interesting when it reflects a conversational tone. Never read directly from notes because it tends to flatten your voice and you also lose eye contact with your audience.

1. Facial expressions

Facial cues are easy to detect. You can communicate interest, pleasure, lack of understanding, or displeasure, depending on whether you smile or frown, especially if you combine it with head movements such as nods or shakes, or if you tilt your head and ear toward someone while looking thoughtful, which shows that you are listening.

You may not always be aware of your own facial expressions, so it could be worth getting feedback on how you come across. Karen, an experienced teacher, did not understand why her students felt intimidated by her at times. When she participated in an instructional techniques workshop I conducted, her colleagues were able to tell her what she was doing and I also picked up good examples on videotape to show her. Karen is a very keen teacher; when students made comments or answered her questions, she would walk toward them and lean forward so she could concentrate on what they said. What she did not realize, though, was what she thought was a look of interest and concentration on her face was so fierce that it came across as threatening! Combined with her close proximity to the student while she looked like this, it was no wonder that it was interpreted negatively.

We encouraged Karen not to approach students quite so closely and to nod and smile at them while she listened to them, so that she actually communicated what she really intended.

2. Voice modulation

Your voice has great potential for gaining attention, for maintaining interest, and for helping in learning and remembering (often through emphasis). But it can be boring or, at least, overused, if you don't vary it.

(a) Volume

You can go from loud to soft, all the way from shouting to whispering. Often, one of the most effective ways to get attention in a noisy situation is to talk very quietly, which is usually the opposite of what most of us do. You should also vary your volume level for variety.

You obviously need to talk more loudly in a larger room, but this does not mean shouting. Our hearing is more acute at the beginning of the day than it is later and in the evening, so you can talk more softly first thing in the morning.

(b) Pitch

If your pitch varies little, your voice will be monotonous and boring. When you are animated, your pitch rises and your audience becomes more attentive. Use a tape recorder and practice working on your inflection, so that you sound interested and interesting.

(c) Rate

You can talk quickly or slowly, and you can vary your rate. You may need to slow down a little when imparting new or difficult information or making key points, then speed up at noncritical parts of your presentation. Picking up the pace by increasing the talking rate is usually recommended, say, just after lunch (or an evening meal), when it is usually harder to get and keep attention and a slow rate could have a soporific effect on a group. Variety is important. Most of us recognize that someone who speaks slowly can be tedious after a while, but just as bad is listening to someone speaking quickly all the time — like being in the line of fire of a machine gun!

(d) Tone

Your feelings about your subject, your audience, and the situation are evident from the tone of your voice. The pitch and the rate of speaking contribute to this. Keep in mind Bell Telephone's injunction to speak with "a smile in the voice."

(e) Duration

You can talk for a long time without a break, or for a short time. You can vary the length of your "non-stop" oral presentation by interspersing pauses and silence, using audiovisual aids, or getting the participants to talk instead.

3. Movement and change of position

Your physical stance conveys a message to your audience and it is one that you can vary. If you always stand in one place — fixed behind a podium or a table for example, your audience will get tired of looking at the same spot all the time. It is good for them to change their focus and move their heads and their bodies from time to time because this keeps them more attentive and alert. When you remain behind a podium or a table, you put a physical barrier between you and the group. Moving around adds variety and brings you literally closer to your group.

The way you move is significant. You can move toward someone who is making a comment to indicate your interest, then stand still and look thoughtful, for instance, with your hand under your chin. This way you show that you are really listening.

A good way to get the attention of those who seem to be "tuning out" is to move toward them and continue with what you are saying while standing beside, or behind, them.

4. Gestures

Gestures can augment what you are saying or can be used without words and still be full of meaning.

Pointing to a part of your visual aid focuses attention on that particular element. You can point to someone, smiling and nodding, to elicit a response; or you can point from one person to another to ask for a comment on the first person's response.

Moving your hands in a circular motion and smiling and nodding when someone is speaking can indicate that you want him or her to continue. Holding your hands out, palms upward, while looking expectantly at someone, usually indicates that you are asking: "Is there anything else?"

Holding your arm out with your hand up and palm out is the "stop" cue. If you use this, you should combine it with a smile to be less threatening, especially if you want to have one person answer at a time, have someone reconsider a wrong answer, or to deter a dominant participant from always answering.

5. Silence

Most presenters know that effective verbal communication is a vital skill, but often they do not include silence in this skill area. Indeed, many people feel uncomfortable with silence and may need to practice using it intentionally. Silence works best when it is perceived as friendly and non-threatening, perhaps accompanied by an indication of pleasure, acceptance, or questioning. Silence can be used to provide —

(a) contrast — periods of speaking interspersed with pauses;

(b) time for something to "sink in." It also indicates that what has just been said is important and worth remembering.

(c) time for thinking and responding (e.g., when you are asking questions); and

(d) an indication of interest — silence says, "Tell me more," especially when accompanied by a smile or a nod.

b. PUTTING YOURSELF AT GREATEST ADVANTAGE

The initial impression you make should establish your credibility and sincerity and make your audience feel it is worth listening to you. Remember the well-known maxim: "You never get a second chance to make a first impression." If the first impression you create is negative, it can be extremely difficult to recover from it. The first two minutes are critical in setting the tone.

First and foremost, you want to be early, ready, organized, in control, looking and acting right. Take the time to greet as many people as you can, with a smile and with a firm, but friendly handshake. It may be worth going to the washroom beforehand to wash and dry your hands, so you can avoid sweaty palms and shake hands with comfort. (I particularly do this in winter, so I can warm up my hands, too!)

Be confident and positive and look at your entire audience immediately when you begin. Your confidence is also expressed in the way you sit, stand and walk, as well as in the kinds of gestures you make (broad rather than tight and close to your body).

Don't forget your physical appearance. Professionalism demands that you should always be well groomed. Your dress must fit the group's expectations and the organization and geographic culture. Be rather conservative in dress and manner unless this is definitely not required. Avoid distracting accessories such as jewelry, especially if is noisy when you move (e.g., bracelets), and do not play with watches, earrings, or anything else!

It goes without saying that you should maintain the highest standards of personal hygiene. Tension can cause increased perspiration: use an effective deodorant and wear lighter clothes or dress in layers so you can take off a jacket, if this is acceptable.

Use a mouthwash, and do not wear strong perfume, cologne, or after-shave. Not only are these distracting, but many people are allergic to certain fragrances.

Establish an assertive physical presence by using relaxed expansive movements: use your space liberally. Try to keep an erect, relaxed posture, but stand your ground. When you take a firm stance, you communicate confidence, that you are a strong individual, and that you can't be pushed around. Do not keep shifting position and do not take lots of small steps. On the other hand, do not restrict your movements by standing with your legs pushed together.

Don't smile unless you really want to. This is especially important for women, since they tend to smile much more than men do. It does not help their credibility level at all if they smile when it's inappropriate.

Similarly, be careful about laughing, especially just before or just after saying something. This is often a sign of nervousness and can detract from your credibility.

Besides looking confident, you want to sound confident. Before your presentation begins, prepare your voice so you are ready to speak, not squeak. Keep a glass of water handy, too, just in case. Consider the following points as you warm up your voice:

(a) Practice breathing deeply so that your abdomen and back muscles respond to your breath.

(b) Test for shallow breathing: look in a mirror when you breathe. If your shoulders rise as you inhale, and fall as you exhale, you are using shallow "chest breathing."

(c) Use more low pitches when speaking. Breath support helps, as does singing, or reciting poems. Hum frequently when alone to exercise the vocal chords.

(d) Project your voice energetically. This does not just mean being loud; it is not the volume itself which matters, but being able to breathe correctly. When you breathe deeply and use your abdomen and back for breath support, you can expel your words so well that they reach an audience at the back of the room.

(e) Do not end sentences on an upward pitch. This makes statements sound like questions and undermines your look of confidence.

c. "A FUNNY THING HAPPENED TO ME…": USING HUMOR

Most adults appreciate a lighter touch, especially if the subject matter is somewhat dry, and humor can certainly help keep your audience's attention. Humor releases the tension, turns learning into fun, and usually increases creativity as well as opening people up to the possibility of change.

Humor can take several forms. You can use cartoons in slides, overheads, and handouts. You can relate funny anecdotes and one-liners. You can even make up humorous names for case studies. Many training films and videos use humor to increase interest and to make their points more meaningful and memorable. My favorite ones are made by John Cleese's company, Video Arts. Cleese has produced a good selection of videos and films on topics such as finance, managing people, decision making, and meeting management. I have found that they are very popular and deliver their message well. Most people relate to these and understand the "how not to" approach as well as the "how to" methods.

Quotations, ideas, and stories from books written especially for speakers can be a good source of material. Build up your own file from what you may read in newspapers, see on signs, overhear, be told, or think of. For example, in courses I run on written communication, I often show examples of signs many of us have seen to illustrate how we *mis*communicate without realizing it. These include —

- Bus Stop — No standing

- Baby Sale on Fourth Floor

- All clothing reduced

However, if you aren't comfortable with humor, don't force it into your presentation. You do not need to be a stand-up comic (it is much better not to be one), and you are not there for pure entertainment or to do a song and dance act and provoke gales of laughter. Never *work* at injecting a note of humor into the proceedings. This comes across as false, especially if it does not fit with your natural style.

I witnessed a very clear example of false humor in a series of workshops I conducted some time ago. As part of the program for a client, I invited one of their own internal experts to talk to the group. After being introduced, he told a joke and the group laughed politely. Then he made his presentation, which was very well re-

ceived. He was knowledgeable and obviously keen to pass on his knowledge to others, but it was also clear that he was a serious sort of a person and telling jokes was not normal for him. Afterwards, the group said he should definitely be invited back for the next group's program. On that occasion, he again started with a joke; not the same as the other one, but not quite as good. This time the laughter was rather more polite. The presentation was as good as before and was equally well received. It seemed to me that someone had told him that telling a joke was a good way to break the ice before making a presentation. But for him it was very forced, since it was not his natural style at all, and it actually had the opposite effect, making the group feel uncomfortable. He had no need to do that because his credibility and interest soon became apparent and everyone adjusted well to his low-key, more serious approach.

It goes without saying that nobody should ever be offensive or make jokes or funny remarks at the expense of others, or tell stories that are in questionable taste. Be aware of the composition of your audience, the gender mix, even their ethnic or cultural background. This is not only so that you can avoid offending anyone, but also so that you can consider the cultural differences in what people would find funny. Again, when in doubt, leave it out!

d. ATTENTION GRABBERS

"Stimulus variation" refers to ways of gaining and maintaining attention and interest. Some examples include the following:

(a) *Surprise* — interest is increased by introducing the unexpected into the session. An unannounced guest speaker might provide a pleasant surprise.

(b) *Novelty* — a new situation will engage your audience's attention.

(c) *Conflict* — the tension generated by conflict can maintain attention until the conflict is resolved. I use this method regularly when I ask groups to report back with their decisions after a case study and their suggestions or solutions conflict. These reports are all received without comment until the end, when we discuss the merits of each and reach consensus on a preferred solution.

(d) *Complexity* — attention increases with the intricacy of a situation. It is usually good to go from the simple to the more complex, to build on knowledge and understanding, to increase the timing and processing of information.

(e) *Intensity* — vividness, action, and emotion engage and maintain attention. You can do a lot by being lively, animated, and enthusiastic as well as by using videos or films that are vivid and action oriented.

(f) *Uncertainty* — ambiguity and ambivalence can help to spark interest if used well. By presenting, for example, questions or problems to be considered that do not have a clear answer, participants have to think and reason and stay involved.

(g) *Variety* — alternating instruction and delivery methods and activities prevents boredom.

(h) *Duration and repetition* — we all need some variety to learn. No matter how good some techniques might be, they lose their effectiveness if they go on too long or the same ones are used repeatedly.

You can incorporate one or more of these strategies when you begin with a problem on which to focus and encourage the consideration of choices before arriving at a solution to stimulate divergent thinking and problem solving. Attention-producing cues can steer learners in the desired direction. For example:

(a) *Verbal focusing* — Use spoken cues like "Listen to this," or "Watch what happens." Emphasize with voice stress, intonation, and volume

(b) *Gesture focusing* — Use simple gestures like pointing

You can also shift sensory channels by emphasizing another sense. Of the five senses — hearing, sight, touch, smell, and taste — hearing is overused in presentations. You need to appeal to the other senses as well. Whenever it's appropriate, for example, take your audience from ears to eyes, from listening to manipulating objects, from watching you demonstrate a task to practicing it. Such shifts alert the information-processing parts of the brain.

Vary the pace by changing methods, say from more passive to more active involvement. Initially this will encourage attention: later it will encourage reflective thinking. Consider your timing: What time of day is it? What are the fatigue factors for your group?

Change the styles of interaction. Switch from trainer/trainee interactions to trainee/trainee interactions. Have your trainees do a role-play exercise. Put them in small groups, in pairs, or have them do independent work.

e. PRACTICE MAKES PERFECT

You should practice making your presentation before doing it for real. In his book, *Making Successful Presentations*, Terry Smith outlines three necessary stages in practicing:

(a) practicing on your own;

(b) a dry run in front of people; and

(c) a rehearsal, or final run-through, where you simulate the final situation as closely as possible.

1. Practice

This is what you can do on your own, in front of the mirror, into a tape recorder.

(a) Read your script aloud, underline words and phrases, mark pauses, leave out difficult words and ones that don't sound so good.

(b) Tape yourself using your script.

(c) Listen to the tape and make improvements. Repeat steps (b) and (c) as needed.

2. Dry run

This is your first try in front of real people. Use associates, friends, or family.

(a) Give them the background on your presentation, the audience, and your objectives.

(b) Give your presentation, explain where and how you would use audiovisual aids. Have them act as your audience; let them time and evaluate your presentation.

(c) Ask for evaluation and constructive criticism at the end. Use the criticism to make improvements.

3. Rehearsal

This is your final run-through, so reproduce the conditions you will face at the actual presentation as much as possible. It is a dress rehearsal, so consider your appearance.

(a) Try to use the actual room, even try for the same time of day.

(b) Use the equipment you will be using; use your audiovisuals.

(c) Be careful about your timing. Fit a question and answer time in, too.

(d) Get your audience to evaluate you on the presentation: the content of your presentation, your voice, your manner, (i.e., your nonverbal signals), and your use of audiovisuals.

(e) Make any necessary improvements.

Samples #13 and #14 show evaluation forms that can be used as tools for your rehearsals. In Sample #13, you evaluate yourself after your practice session. It allows you to focus on many different aspects of your total presentation.

Then, you might use the feedback sheet in Sample #14 for your trial audience. Ask your audience to comment on each of the categories, particularly on areas where you need to improve. For example, someone might write that you need to work on "pacing." In discussion, or from what they write on the evaluation form, you might discover that there are times you need to slow down your presentation. For each part of these forms, elicit comments on how well you are doing, what strengths to build on, where you need to improve, and how to accomplish that, if possible.

Once you've practiced a few times, you're ready to go. But you should use a last-minute checklist to make sure you haven't forgotten anything. Before a presentation, run through Checklist #2.

Read these statements carefully, and for each one circle the number that indicates how often the statement applies to your presentations.

Use this scale: 1 = Never   2 = Rarely   3 = Sometimes   4 = Often   5 = Always

My rating:	ITEM:
1 2 ③ 4 5	I set well-defined objectives simply and quickly.
1 2 3 ④ 5	Before presentations, I identify audience needs simply and quickly.
1 2 3 ④ 5	I put my material in the best sequence I can to have the most impact on those who must be persuaded.
1 2 3 ④ 5	I anticipate audience questions when preparing my presentations.
1 2 3 4 ⑤	I request constructive feedback from others about my presentations (from colleagues, for example).
1 ② 3 4 5	I give my audiences an agenda at the start.
1 2 ③ 4 5	I develop audience interest at the start.
1 2 ③ 4 5	I really emphasize points that my audience may have difficulty accepting.
1 2 3 ④ 5	I maintain rapport with audiences when answering their questions.
1 ② 3 4 5	I deal constructively with resistance from my audience.
1 2 3 ④ 5	My presentations motivate my audiences to take immediate action.
1 ② 3 4 5	I maintain a continuing dialogue with my audience.
1 2 3 ④ 5	The structure of my presentations makes them easy to deliver and follow.
1 2 3 ④ 5	My closings are designed to help my audience retain the major points.
1 2 ③ 4 5	I use words that are appropriate for my audience. *Don't always really know!*
1 ② 3 4 5	I control my nervousness.
1 2 ③ 4 5	I use my tone of voice to emphasize the content.
1 2 ③ 4 5	I maintain a friendly tone of voice throughout.
1 ② 3 4 5	I use my facial expressions and physical gestures to emphasize the content.

? 1 2 ③ 4 5   I project a positive attitude.

? 1 2 ③ 4 5   I demonstrate my personal credibility.

   1 2 3 ④ 5   The visual aids I use provide powerful reinforcement to my major points.

   1 ② 3 4 5   I reflect carefully after the presentation on how I did, and I think how to build on my strengths and what and how to improve.

NOTES

What I should work on to improve my presentations

PREPARATION / BEFOREHAND

> Relax!
> Work out what resistance is likely and how to handle it
> Think about language used (?)

DURING THE PRESENTATION

> Very clear agenda at the beginning
> Have more interaction
> Need to be more animated — better voice, interest perhaps related to relaxing

AFTERWARDS

> More self-evaluation — also ask others for feedback?
> (Perhaps I should videotape myself to check on some of this?)

FEEDBACK ON STRUCTURE AND ILLUSTRATION

Comments

THE OPENING

- Rapport statement — *?*
- Reference to problem, issue, opportunity — *GOOD*
- Credentials — *OK*
- Agenda — *— NEED TO SPELL OUT WHAT & HOW*
- Request for action — *YES*
- Bridge to body — *OK*
- Overall evaluation of opening — *BE A BIT MORE SPECIFIC & BE MORE FRIENDLY AT START*

THE BODY

- Introduction — *✓*
- Proofs — *✓ } GOOD USE SLIDES HERE*
- Recap proofs, conclusions — *✓*
- Solicit audience response — *NEED TO GET MORE*
- Bridge to closing — *✓*
- Overall evaluation of body — *OK*

THE CLOSING

- Restate problem — *✓*
- Restate agenda — *— DIDN'T*
- Restate request for action — *BE MORE FIRM HERE*
- Overall evaluation of closing — *OK*

EMOTION APPEALS

- Hot words
- Message appeals — *} NOT "EMOTIONAL" REALLY*

ILLUSTRATIONS — *GOOD SLIDES & EXAMPLES*

OTHER COMMENTS: NEED TO BE MORE "HUMAN," THOUGH. ALSO GET RESPONSE/INTERACTION SO YOU CAN USE INFORMATION AUDIENCE MIGHT GIVE YOU.

FEEDBACK ON DELIVERY

Comments

WORDS AND TONE OF VOICE

- Clear language
- Enunciation
- Pacing
- Varied tone of voice

 GOOD

NOT A LOT

BODY LANGUAGE

- Mannerisms
- Pauses, breathing
- Posture
- Attitude projected

 OK

A BIT STIFF
RATHER SERIOUS

RAPPORT

- Eye contact
- Made audience feel comfortable
- Earned respect

TRY TO LOOK AT EVERYONE

NEED TO SMILE MORE!

CREDIBILITY

- Words
- Tone of voice
- Body language
- Balanced perspective
- Ethical behavior
- Flexibility

YES
✓

A BIT STIFF

✓

HANDLING QUESTIONS

- Listening
- Paraphrasing
- Ensured response was satisfactory
- Dealt with difficult questions

GOOD: NODDING, ETC.
✓
DIDN'T CHECK ENOUGH HERE
SEEMED A BIT ANXIOUS AT TIMES

GENERAL COMMENTS ON DELIVERY

NEED TO RELAX MORE!

CHECKLIST #2
BEFORE A SPEECH OR PRESENTATION

☐ Check your notes or script. Are they in proper order? Secure them together, but don't staple them (you'll just have to take the staples out later). Rubber bands work for cards; large paper clips work for both cards and pages.

☐ Put your notes into your pocket, purse, or briefcase. If possible, have a duplicate set very close by.

☐ Is all audiovisual material in order?

☐ Do you have additional bulbs, extension cords, etc.?

☐ Take your security blankets (aspirins, handkerchief, extra pantyhose, glasses, extra glasses). Remember Murphy's Law.

☐ Check the news. Does it affect or influence your speech or presentation? Be ready to incorporate or change.

☐ If you are making an in-house presentation, take a pulse reading of your company. Very recent decisions could affect your presentation. Be aware of what is going on.

☐ Check to see that there have been no last-minute changes in the program or agenda.

☐ If you're making your presentation with someone else, allow time to meet and make final reassurances.

☐ Arrive early.

☐ Check the setup of the room. Rearrange if necessary.

☐ Test the microphone if you will be using one.

☐ Set up audiovisual material.

☐ Check to make sure equipment is working.

☐ If using slides, run through quickly as a final check that they're in order.

☐ Check for distractions. People will read and re-read any printed material on the walls. Take down posters. If you speak after someone else, be sure all his or her visuals have been removed before you speak.

☐ Make a final visit to the washroom. Make sure your hair is well-groomed at the back as well as the front. If you speak after a meal, check your teeth and brush them if possible.

☐ Tuck in shirttails all around, button all buttons, and zipper all zippers.

☐ If you need water at the lectern, check to see that it is there. Don't rely on someone else to get it.

7 Speaker for hire: the business of seminars

As a professional with special expertise, you might now, or in the future, want to concentrate more of your efforts on working with clients or spending more time conducting seminars or running programs. The information in this chapter will help you plan. It covers some of the special considerations for those who want to make a business out of giving seminars.

a. SELECTING TOPICS

What you offer clients for presentations, talks, workshops, or seminars will be based mainly on your own areas of expertise, specialized knowledge, and skills. But if you are in the seminar business for the long haul, you have to be able to adapt your expertise and areas of interest to the changing demands of the market. You should also anticipate potential needs by being aware of —

(a) emerging market trends,

(b) the state of the economy and its effects on your clients,

(c) new technology,

(d) new legal requirements, and

(e) new knowledge, techniques, and skills that will be needed.

As an example, if you regularly run seminars on how to start a business, you need to keep abreast of the legal setting in which you are operating, any changes, and how these would affect your target audience. Changing tax laws could affect business owners, so you would have to update your content and materials accordingly.

b. PROMOTION AND MARKETING

If running seminars is your business, much of your time will be spent marketing your service. You might distribute professionally produced brochures, or put together your own promotional literature if you have high-quality computer facilities. You can send this sort of material direct to clients, to relevant professional groups and organizations, to conference and seminar organizers, and to referrals, as well as giving or sending your literature to anyone who attends one of your presentations.

You will probably get the best results from people who already know you and what you can do. Your credibility will be enhanced if you can mention the name of a satisfied customer.

Here are some suggestions to help you consider the types of information you could include in your marketing promotions:

- *Title:* Choose a dynamic title that reflects the level and focus of your topic. Dynamic titles include words that grab attention and generate interest in attending, for example: "Essentials of ..."; "An Introduction to ..."; "A Basic ..." "Understanding ..."; "Improving your ..."; "Effective ... Skills"; "Strategies for ..."; "Secrets of Successful ..." "How to ..."

- *Summary:* A summary of your offering

- *Rationale and general aims:* Reasons for your offering; why it is needed for this particular group at this time; a general overview of the purpose

- *Target audience:* Precisely who this is designed for; a statement of any prerequisites (i.e., any required experience, skills, knowledge, education)

- *Duration and timing:* How many hours or days; one full week or, one day a week for 3 weeks

- *Objectives:* (This is optional.) This section is most relevant for training, and may be required by clients. Objectives express learner outcomes as a result of attending. (See chapter 2 for more on objectives.)

- *Program outline:* This may range from just listing the topics to be covered all the way to a detailed outline in an agenda format, with topics, timing, and even methods used at each stage.

- *Methods:* A brief description of the process.

- *Leader information:* A brief biography, including relevant information on qualifications and work experience and a list of other clients, to establish your credibility. (Clients might use some of your information for their own promotion purposes.)

c. TRAINING CONTRACT OR LETTER OF UNDERSTANDING

Many consultants don't realize the importance of developing a contract or letter of understanding for their seminar business. They may agree to work with a client and just operate on a spoken agreement, as a result of a meeting, or even after a brief discussion on the phone. These casual arrangements can turn into problems if you are ever unfortunate enough to work with clients who do not honor their agreements — or pay their bills!

Forestall problems by putting together your own letter of understanding (see Sample #15). You can send it out on your own letterhead when an agreement has been reached for you to make a presentation, speak at a conference, or conduct a training session. This letter will confirm in writing your understanding of the agreed arrangements, as well as state some of your needs.

Include the date and time of the session, what your fee will be, how you expect payment to be made (e.g., in full after the session, half before the seminar and half after, or some other arrangement), who is responsible for supplying various props, materials, etc. The clearer you can be in a contract or letter of understanding, the less likely you will run into problems.

d. MEETING THE CLIENT'S NEEDS

1. What does your client say is needed?

Find out everything you can about your client. Obtain information about the target audience, including the following:

(a) Who are they? What are their professions or roles and areas of responsibility?

(b) Are they attending willingly?

(c) What are their expectations?

If possible, meet the group or a sampling of the group, or the supervisor or manager, before the session. This way, you can explain what you will do and answer their questions. If you meet the supervisors/managers, you can get their point of view about the group's needs.

If training is requested, ensure that training is the true need; organizations may ask for staff to be trained to do their jobs better, when it is not really lack of knowledge or skills that is causing the deficiency in performance.

You'll find it useful to do a needs assessment (see chapter 2). When you meet with your contact person or with the group you can ask —

(a) What "problems" need solving?

(b) What results are required?

(c) What have prospective participants indicated they want?

(d) What precipitated the client's approach to you?

2. What does the client really want you to do?

Clients may not be able to express clearly what they really want to have happen. You may have to help them work it out. What you are asked to do or what you are told is the problem may not really fit the client's purpose, so you may have to "read between the lines" here.

Possibly what your client wants is a workshop or presentation that will make the audience "feel good," that will give employees high motivation. The client may need you to give more of a pep-talk than pass on needed information.

e. LEARNING CONTRACTS

A client for whom I offer training seminars has an excellent "learning contract" system. Before any seminar, participants complete the contract together with their managers (see Sample #16). Copies of the form are sent to the human resources department, and then one is sent to the seminar leader.

This system ensures that both staff and managers determine real training needs and pass on this information so that these needs are satisfied. It is also quite successful in gaining commitment not only from prospective participants but also from their managers and means that there is more likely to be continued commitment and support afterwards.

f. EVALUATION AND FOLLOW-UP

Evaluation can be done by the participants immediately at the conclusion of your session, and/or at some later time. Supervisors or managers might later evaluate the effectiveness of your session in terms of, for example, improvements in their staff's knowledge, skills, and performance. You might also conduct a follow-up session to discuss the effects of your first session, for example, what participants have implemented or changed as a result (see Samples #7 and #8 in chapter 2 for examples of evaluation questionnaires).

Evaluations are important for feedback, for you and for the client, and follow-up is of great value as an incentive to participants to put ideas into practice as well as test out new learning and report back on its value.

It is always worth discussing your program afterwards with your original contact person. At this stage you might discuss what transpired, based on the evaluations, the results you achieved, any follow-up sessions, etc. This might also be an opportunity to pass on any information, comments, or suggestions you elicited from the group that they wish the organization to know about.

XYZ CONSULTANTS INCORPORATED

LETTER OF UNDERSTANDING

Date: April 1, 19____

To: J. Doe, Bigge Business Ltd.

RE: Computer Training Seminar

This is to confirm that I will offer to the Data Entry Department of your organization, Bigge Business Ltd., a seminar on upgrading Entry Software to version 307.1 from 9 a.m. to 10 a.m., on Monday, April 30, 199-.

The number of participants will be limited to 10.

My fee will be $500 in total.

Cancellation fee: 50% if cancelled within one week before agreed date.

This fee includes:

(a)   Two discussions with you prior to session date and one meeting with group to establish needs

(b)   Developing the session, customizing to suit your specific needs, follow-up/evaluation

(c)   All handout materials
These are only for the use of those attending and are not to be copied for others' use.

(d)   Films/videos and other audiovisual media

It is understood that you/your organization will provide:

(a)   Facilities for the session:
room, refreshments (specify), copying of handouts, and name cards

(b)   List of those attending and relevant details about them

(c) Audiovisual requirements:
☑ overhead projector and screen   ☑ slide projector
☐ video cassette recorder   ☑ flip chart   ☐ other _film projector_

(d) Room setup
☐ boardroom/U-shape   ☐ small tables   ☑ classroom style
☐ speaker's table at the front   ☐ other_____

(e) Contact person during session
Name: _Ima Contact_
Phone number: _604 - 1234_

Yours sincerely,

J. M. Trainer

I. Trainer
XYZ Consultants Inc.

SAMPLE #16
LEARNING CONTRACT

Name of participant: Chris Jackson

Position: Foreman   Department: Maintenance

Summary of responsibilities and duties:

Provide maintenance to Production Dept.
Supervise 5 workers; Scheduling; some training; Reports.

Particular pressures and/or concerns in my job:

- Staff now supervised used to be peer group.
- Conflicting priorities

Workshop planning to attend: 1st Line Supervision Date: July 15

Objectives: What I want to achieve from attending this workshop:

1. How to handle former colleagues as staff.
2. Discipline!
3. Knowledge about legal requirements
4. Running staff meetings

Name of manager/supervisor:

What I wish this staff member to achieve from the workshop:

1. More confidence in being the foreman now.
2. Dealing with people problems - staff
3. Training staff in safety procedures
4.

How I plan to help him/her apply the knowledge/skills gained:

Discuss after course what was learned and help
him put it into practice.

Signed: Chris Jackson _____ (participant) Date: June 30

Signed: A. Brown _____ (manager/supervisor) Date: June 30

Received in Human Resources: RD   Date: June 30/9-

Follow-up action by manager/supervisor and participant:

Meetings — next day and 2 weeks after course and
planned monthly for next 3 months.

8 Conferences, professional organizations, and other large meetings

If you are invited to speak at larger meetings or conferences, you will need to plan in the same way as described throughout this book, but you will also have to be sensitive to the special considerations of this type of presentation. Usually, because of the exposure you will receive, it is of great professional advantage to be a keynote speaker or part of a conference workshop. You can gain a lot of positive P.R. from being featured in a brochure, publication, or in any other media promotion.

When you speak to larger groups in a more formal setting, you may need to modify some aspects of your presentation. This chapter addresses concerns that become especially important when you are communicating to a large audience.

a. THE BIGGER PICTURE

The main difference when speaking at a large conference is that you have less control over content and setting. Usually, you will have to tailor your workshop or speech to the needs of the group, which requires your research into their particular needs and expectations. It may also mean contacting other presenters and working with them so that information given isn't redundant.

If the conference you are asked to speak at is a regular event, you should ask for previous program outlines or brochures. These will give you a good idea what is normal for this type of event and provide some insight into the organizing group, and can help you decide whether you want

to be associated with them. Is appearing with this group a good way to promote yourself?

As with any other presentation, be sure to prepare, get organized, and check out the facility beforehand. Find out whatever you can ahead of time or come early if you can only see the location on the actual day. Walk around the room and figure out where to place things in terms of visibility and ease of use; check the lights, windows, etc. Your professional kit will come in handy for adapting your usual presentations to this specific situation.

Take the time to find out who will be introducing you or assisting you. Pass on any information that you want mentioned, and try to build rapport with the conference organizers.

Incidentally, some professional conference and seminar organizations expect you to promote their materials such as books and videos. First, you should consider whether you can achieve your purpose with the size of group they might stipulate. Second, think about how comfortable you feel taking on a sales role.

I always look at exactly what material is being offered to participants, and decide what, if anything, I can sincerely recommend. Otherwise, I usually mention that there are materials for participants to purchase, if they wish, and merely suggest they look over what is available, without necessarily endorsing anything in particular. Frankly, I think a hard sell turns off most people, and I do not want to be a salesperson. Participants usually take you seriously if you recommend any books, etc., so you must handle any endorsements carefully because it affects your credibility. I do not even push my own books very hard, though I have them available in case I am asked or if people want more information that is contained in my book.

b. YOUR PRESENCE

In front of a large group, you need to be more noticeable, but without being a distraction. If you are on a platform, wear solid-colored clothes that show up well, such as navy suits, and, when appropriate, bright blue or red, for women, but certainly not pastels, brown or beige, nor too-vivid patterns. Also, watch some stripes or checks which appear to "move" as you do.

Find out the color of the stage background. You do not want to blend into it so well that you disappear! Also, people won't listen as well if you clash too much with your background. Again, dark suits with light shirts or blouses work well because the lighter material near your face focuses attention there.

Women might want to wear more defined make-up. However, make-up shouldn't be so intrusive that it adversely affects your professional appearance. Make sure your face is visible, which means paying attention to hair styles and the type of glasses you wear, if any.

You will probably have less time to establish rapport with your audience, so you need to get in there quickly and do this right away. Smile, display confidence, and start with a strong, definite introduction, which will establish you as organized, smart, and ready for action.

c. SPEAKING FROM A PLATFORM

Have everything you need on you or set everything out beforehand on the lectern or a nearby table. Your notes should be in a clearly marked or distinctive folder; don't let the person who has just introduced you walk away with your notes! (It is a good idea to have a duplicate set of notes in a briefcase.) Keep your glass of water away from where you speak; it's an easy thing to knock over even if you don't have an expressive gesturing style.

A rule of thumb is to have at least 18 inches of your head and shoulders easily visible from the platform, so consider how you will use a lectern, if available. If you are short, you can stand to the side of the lectern or use a table for your notes, as long as you do not look down to read them.

Stand quietly for five seconds before starting, then begin clearly and confidently. Don't take any longer than that and don't start to sort your notes or pick up other items, because you will look disorganized or uncaring.

d. EYE CONTACT

You may have heard these two pieces of advice about making eye contact when speaking to large groups —

(a) Locate a point behind and just above the heads of the middle section of your audience and address most of your remarks there, or

(b) Pick out a friendly looking person in the audience and address most of your remarks to him or her.

My response to this is: DON'T!

I have seen members of such an audience look behind them to see what or who the speaker is looking at, since it was obviously not them. The friendly looking person will stop feeling friendly after a while if you continue to single out him or her. The rest of the group will feel left out or that they do not need to listen since you will never notice if they are paying attention or not.

In her book *Speak Like a Pro*, Margaret Bedrosian categorizes four effective forms of eye contact. She advises that at least three of these should make up 90% of your presentation.

    (a) Glance at the audience. Look up periodically for sentences, full phrases, or stories, especially if you are reading from a text.

    (b) Divide the room into quarters. Draw invisible mental lines back to front and side to side along the room, quartering it. Consciously address each of the four quarters periodically, so that no group gets left out of eye contact.

    (c) Sweep the audience. Sweep means you scan a row in a horizontal movement, reaching many people briefly.

    (d) Hold your gaze. Maintain contact with one person for six seconds or one full sentence, whichever is longer. This is one of the most effective forms of eye contact since focusing attention on individuals in a large audience makes everyone feel involved. It also gives you the opportunity to read a few faces every minute or so in greater depth. However, as I just pointed out, this does not mean picking only one or two people.

Do not focus on the ones who are looking hostile, perhaps sitting with their arms tightly crossed. Rather, look at those who smile, nod, or seem interested and encouraging.

e. READING YOUR NOTES

Do not simply read your notes out aloud. Most people feel quite insulted when this is done to them, feeling that they would just as soon be given the "speech" and read it themselves, perhaps over a cup of coffee in more comfortable surroundings.

When you read anything, you look downwards, so all that's visible is the top of your head. You lose eye contact with your group, which turns them off and cancels any opportunity you might have had to check their reactions to what you are saying. Your voice also goes downwards, rather than forwards, and your tone will probably flatten out and become far less interesting. All of this puts more distance between you and your audience.

By all means, have good notes to which you can refer easily, but this does not mean having a speech written out in full sentences that you read verbatim. That is the situation in more formal lectures and talks, but it's not what works best for most audiences.

f. USING A MICROPHONE

Decide whether to use a microphone and request one if needed. It can help you speak more naturally, or even softly, in larger groups and should not get in your way once you are used to using one. A good rule of thumb to follow is that you should use a microphone when speaking to any group of more than 125 people, when the majority of the audience is over 55 years old, and where the room layout or acoustics make it advisable (and if your voice is strained).

If there is a fixed microphone on a lectern, you must match it to your height. It is best at one or two inches below your chin and six to nine inches in front of you so that you can speak across the top of the microphone. This means your whole face is visible and you avoid the hiss of the "s" and the noisy breath of letters such as "t" and "p."

A fixed microphone also fixes you in place, so you must try to be even more expressive and use gestures to compensate for your lack of movement. If you can and wish to unhook the microphone and walk around holding it, this is worth practicing.

The battery-operated, wireless type of microphone is best — if you have a choice — because it allows you to move easily and freely. However, you are more likely to be offered the lavaliere, or lapel, type. This small microphone clips to your clothing and is wired to the sound system. (Women will have to plan to wear something it will clip to and avoid jewelry that can "clunk" against it.) You should practice walking around wearing this and how to avoid tripping or being caught in the wire. It is much better than a fixed microphone since it allows you to move around and be more visible and interesting.

Whenever you are using a microphone, test it ahead of time to ensure it is working. When speaking into it, speak normally. Don't tap it or say "testing, testing" once your session has begun. Assume it is working well unless you see that members of your audience are obviously having problems hearing you.

g. SELECTING YOUR METHOD

Deciding what method to use will be determined mainly by what it is you are trying to achieve. You may give a speech to pass on information, to impress or motivate a group, or even for entertainment, particularly if you have been asked to make an after-dinner speech. You may read a paper at a meeting of a professional organization. In these instances, you will speak to the audience directly in a one-way communication style.

I often train hairdressers who want to be instructors in hairdressing schools. They attend hairdressing shows where they are part of a large audience watching a professional demonstrate interesting or new techniques. These demonstrations are often less for instruction than for impressing others with the demonstrator's expertise and innovation and to introduce new hair-care products. When you are more concerned with helping others learn or develop skills or knowledge, you will use methods appropriate to your purpose (see chapter 4), such as the following:

- Lectures

- Illustrated talks/presentations

- Interactive methods, where this is desirable and the group size and the facilities permit

Lectures and illustrated talks, especially when accompanied by audiovisual aids, work well with large groups. Participants can learn through interaction such as questions and answers and discussion.

With larger groups, you may want to provide handouts ahead of time rather than during the meeting to avoid disrupting the flow of your presentation while papers are passed and shuffled. Alternatively, if you prefer to hand out material during the presentation, ask for help in distributing any paper so that minimal disruption occurs.

h. AUDIOVISUAL AIDS

Whether you use any audiovisual aids is determined by group size. It is not appropriate to use flipcharts or boards with larger groups, and videotapes will not work unless there are multiple monitors or large screens. Usually, slides and overhead projectors work well, as long as the visuals are large and clear enough and the lighting is appropriate (preferably dimmed lights, rather than too-bright lighting, or total darkness) and screens don't distort the image. Before using anything, check out the visibility yourself, and make sure equipment is placed where you want it and can use it easily. Use a lighted pointer for slides on the screen.

i. ROOM ARRANGEMENTS

You may have little choice in how the room is arranged for a large presentation, but find out if there is any flexibility. If you can, arrange seats and tables to maximize the learning experience.

Sample #17 shows the kind of list you might want to use if you are asked to speak

Conference/meeting: *Annual Conference for Chartered Accountants*

Working title (if any):

Usual promotion/publicity outlets: *Professional Journal, Chapters of Professional Association*

Other sessions and speakers planned:

My sessions:

Topic(s) and/or Title(s): *How to Make Effective Presentations*

Format: (e.g., large or small group presentation workshop) *Workshop*

Date(s): *Feb 2nd*

Time(s): *9am – 12 noon*

Breaks: *10:15 – 10:30*

Fee/expenses/other: (include accommodation if needed) *$500 all inclusive*

Cancellation notice and any recompensation: *None*

Location: *Four Seasons Hotel*

Details of those expected to attend

Total expected: *250*   Number for my session(s): *30 max.*

Where from: national   local *✓*   regional *✓*

Who are the prospective attendees? (e.g., typical job titles, professional affiliations):

Chartered Accountants (Comptrollers, P.C.A.)

Their expectations/objectives:

Want to know how to make a presentation to clients, boards, internal colleagues.

Name of overall coordinator: Maria Brodowski

Name of my contact person (if different): ✓

Introducer/assistant available on-site: To be arranged

Handouts:

Printing available: When required: Format:

✓   Min. 3 weeks   Camera ready
                             beforehand

Audiovisual equipment availability:

Requested: Overhead projector and screen

Speaker/session Information:

When required: Format:

2 months beforehand   B + W photograph and
                             1 paragraph bio

Room arrangements available:

small tables

Registration facilities:

Exhibits, publication/speakers' table for promotion etc.?

Yes

at a larger meeting. It covers the main areas of concern for your planning.

j. QUESTIONS AND ANSWERS

Be prepared for questions. People ask questions for genuine reasons, either —

    (a) to gain information, clarification, or help,

    (b) to be helpful, make their own comments, or add something,

    (c) to test you (this may not necessarily be hostile),

    (d) to embarrass you, put you on the spot or hurt you, or

    (e) to get attention, show off, or gain approval.

Your concern generally will not be why they ask questions, but how you handle them.

1. Anticipate questions

Before the session, list all questions you can think of and plan answers for them. Think of some general ones that you can use to get the audience started or make sure everyone understands. For example, you might begin by saying, "A question I am often asked at this point is...." Then observe the group's reactions: you might well see nods and other signs of recognition.

Sample #18 shows how you can plan for any anticipated questions.

2. When and how to answer

It is usually better to answer questions during the presentation as you go along. This is less stressful for you and will help establish rapport with your audience. If you handle points when they come up, confusing issues are clarified immediately. Merely asking "Any questions?" at the end won't work nearly as well. You want to engage your audience and get them to respond to the information you are presenting. You want two-way communication.

However, handling questions throughout a session requires your ability to stay in control of your timing and of where the discussion leads. You don't want the group going off on a tangent and losing your focus. If you plan to allow questions as you speak, be sure to calculate extra time during your planning. Keep an eye on the clock, and don't be afraid to stay in control by politely interrupting and saying, "Perhaps we will have an opportunity to discuss that issue further at the break. I'd like to move on to the next section now...."

You'll be better prepared for handling questions if you keep in mind the following:

    (a) Tell the audience at the beginning that you will answer any questions and when you would prefer them, whether it is as you go along, or at the end, or whatever. Also state exactly how long you will allow for questions if you plan them for the end of your session, and stick to that time. When the time limit expires, you could announce, "We have time for one more question...."

    (b) When pausing to answer a question, mark your place in your presentation so you can pick up where you left off.

    (c) Receive all questions and comments courteously and with patience.

    (d) Use the opportunity to clarify or even to repeat or emphasize points.

    (e) Listen carefully and show you are listening: smile and nod, reflect, restate, and summarize.

    (f) Keep eye contact with the questioner at the start of your answer.

    (g) Rephrase or repeat the question before answering it. This gives you time and allows everyone to hear and understand the question.

    (h) When you forget what was asked or you are uncertain of the answer ask the questioner to rephrase it "so everyone is clear on it," or ask others to respond first. You might say "What do the rest of you think about that?"

(i) Think before answering. Give short answers that are to the point; delay if you must.

(j) Stay in control, do not be defensive; decide if you really want to answer now or at all.

(k) Consider your body language when you listen and answer. Do you come across as interested, or defensive, offensive, or hostile?

(l) If you do not know the answer, have a memory lapse, or do not have enough information at this moment, say so, and offer to get back to the questioner — and make sure you do so!

(m) When questions go off topic, into more depth than you wish to deal with right now, or you feel it is otherwise not appropriate to answer them at this point, feel free to delay giving an immediate answer. Some ways to do this might include saying, "I believe your question will be answered later by what I have to say; get back to me if you still need to."

"Can we hold that until next time?";

"Perhaps we should talk about that together at break time..."

"That's a good question, but not quite what we're dealing with right now." (Then move on.)

(n) Always smile and sound friendly when you use delaying strategies.

Using the Food Guide

Questions:

Answer (+ benefits, if relevant)

1. How can I lose weight if I eat the required no. of servings from each food group?

2. How can I get my family to eat more of the Food Guide foods, esp. vegetables?

3. What about snack foods like potato chips?

4. What if I can't have foods from all the food groups on any given day?

1. Food Guide recommends foods that are nutritious, not high in calories or fat.

2. Offer to supply recipes at end or at another point in lecture; have a handout of recipes.

3. High in fat and calories, so use in moderation

4. Amount of food you need depends on age, size, and activity level. Stress on balance, getting a balance of foods.

General Questions

Answer

1. Are crash diets bad? Liquid-only diets?

2. Which food group does ice cream fall into?

3. What about dessert?

4. Are foods outside the 4 food groups bad?

1. Talk about what the body needs; crash diets mean you regain weight faster.

2. Dairy / milk product. Also high in fat and calories.

3. Recipes with fresh fruit; other recipes from the guide (handout)

4. We can also enjoy these foods; some are higher in fat and calories. Stress moderation. Give examples of variety within the 4 groups. (Will cover in more detail in next session.)

9 Dealing with problems

Nobody wants to think about the things that can go wrong when preparing for a presentation or seminar, but planning for the possibility of problems often means preventing disaster.

There are three basic types of problems you may run up against: problems with other people's behavior, problems with your own behavior, and problems with objects or the environment.

We have already talked at length about tackling many of the problems that can occur with equipment and facilities — the basic message is, anticipate as many eventualities as you can and prepare for them as best you can! Some, like the burnt-out projector lamp, are easy to deal with if you have thought ahead. Others, like a fire alarm going off in the middle of your presentation, are more challenging. These sorts of unexpected events defy preparation, but, at the least, remember always that you are in charge and should try to maintain control of the situation, and that a cool head and professionalism can get you through a lot of things.

a. PROBLEM PEOPLE

Any behavior that interferes with the learning process or disturbs you and/or other participants can be categorized as a problem. Unless the problem is handled well and promptly, it may become "infectious" so that others start to behave in a similar, undesirable fashion. Behavior like this can also create an unsettled atmosphere in the group, lower motivation, or apathy and make participants lose respect for you.

Therefore, you should deal with any problem as soon as possible. This way you minimize any negative effects and prevent something more serious from developing.

If you pay attention to participants, you can pick up both verbal and non-verbal signals that can tell you if have lost the group or the focus of the meeting. The chart in Sample #19 shows the signs to watch for and suggests ways to deal with them.

When considering problematic behavior patterns, it is worth distinguishing between those who are fairly well meaning but something of a problem, and those who are, unfortunately, not well meaning at all! This can affect how you respond to them and how well they respond to suggestions and comments from you and others.

Never be sarcastic or embarrass the problem person in front of everyone else. Although this may be very tempting, it will rarely solve anything; rather, it might make things worse since that person will probably seek revenge! Even if the other participants sympathize with your situation, they will feel uncomfortable when they see you treat someone this way and they may switch their sympathies to the person who is the cause of the problem. Remember, adults expect professionalism from you and this includes the way you handle problems.

Let us look at some of the more common categories of difficult participants, the fairly typical behaviors you might encounter, and some helpful strategies for dealing with them. Bear in mind, though, that these types are not necessarily separate from

Inattentive participants will —

Fidget and shift in their chairs

Let their eyes wander

Slump back in the chair as opposed to leaning forward

Jump ahead in manuals or handouts or read them rather than listen to you

To recapture attention you can —

Shift from lecture to workshop format

Invite questions

Increase variety in your voice: tone, rate, volume, pitch

Invite a member of the group to contribute

If the leader is causing anxiety, the participants will —

Raise the pitch of their voices

Experience voice tremors

Physically withdraw by pushing their chairs away from the table

To relieve anxiety you should —

Ask what is causing the anxiety and talk openly about it

When conflicts are unproductive, participants will —

Use "us-against-them" language. Instead of saying that the group has a problem, they'll say, "I'm right and you're wrong."

Use negative terms. Instead of saying, "I disagree," they'll say, "That's stupid."

Make "global" statements typified by words and phrases such as, "All the time, always." Saying "You always do that" makes an issue global rather than specific.

To solve unproductive conflicts, you can —

Ask the major combatants to reverse roles

Ask the major combatants to back off from the discussion

When the group is not functioning on its own, but is over-dependent on the leader, the participants will: —

Raise their hands instead of jumping into the discussion

Be over-polite: avoid interrrupting one another

To encourage groups to be self-functioning, you can —

Make up an excuse to leave the room

Let the participants lead. Keep the discussion on track, but try not to dominate.

each other; some people can fall into one or more of the categories.

1. Disruptives

Disruptive people may —

(a) come in late, and do not just slip in quietly;

(b) frequently interrupt what you and others say; they are "chatterboxes"; or

(c) distract everyone by having private conversations and talking to each other.

Some people are deliberately disruptive because they seek attention. Here are some strategies for dealing with them:

(a) Never pander to their needs so that they are then rewarded for their disruptive behavior.

(b) Do not notice or comment on lateness when it happens. Later, ask the person alone politely but firmly to come on time or to come in quietly so as not to disrupt the session.

Sometimes, people do not intend to be disruptive, but their personal style or past experience makes them behave in a disruptive way. For unintentional disruptives, try these strategies:

(a) Ask them, in a friendly way, not to have their own separate conversations, or to try to be on time, or come in quietly. You may do this when it happens, but do not make a big issue of it or embarrass anyone.

(b) To keep interruptions down, establish the ground rule that whoever is talking must be allowed to finish before comments are made. This also sharpens everyone's listening skills.

2. Negatives

Negative people may —

(a) squash any attempt at creativity. They will drain everyone's morale and motivation if they're allowed to continue in their usual negative way.

(b) resist change; they respond negatively to others' ideas. They act like "wet blankets."

(c) tell you that something will not work and why; or

(d) complain and always point out problems. They will tell you what is wrong with a situation, usually just dumping the problem. Even if they do come up with any ideas or suggestions for what should be done to rectify the problem, it is usually what others should do, never what they might do. They rarely, if ever, accept responsibility themselves for correcting a situation.

Again, you can combat those negative resisters by invoking the rule that everyone's ideas, suggestions, and comments have to be heard before being countered. Negative responses, including "Yes but..," are not allowed until after participants have come up with all the positive aspects of the ideas. Negative people always find the negative aspects of anything first, so must be encouraged — or forced! — to look for any positives before falling into their automatic negative response pattern.

When participants complain, listen to what they have to say. You don't have to agree with them, but do not argue. Without apology, acknowledge what they say, then switch to problem solving. Ask what they would like to happen, and what they can and will do. Offer to do something yourself, if this is appropriate.

If the same complaints are endlessly repeated, with no suggestions or commitment to do anything, cut off this behavior quickly and firmly whenever it recurs. Just say "This does not seem to be getting us any further ahead; I suggest we should move on, now...," for example.

3. Dominants

Dominant people may —

(a) monopolize discussions and cause resentment and frustration in other participants;

(b) debate and argue with you in order to demonstrate their superiority; or

(c) try to take over from you and diminish your authority.

Some people may have more knowledge than you do in a particular area. For genuinely smart people, recognize their expertise and welcome their useful comments. You can anticipate and prevent them making their comments (or answering all the questions) by smiling at the dominator, then prefacing questions with a remark such as: "How about we hear from someone different for a change?" and look in another direction when asking your questions. If you still get the dominant one chiming in, interrupt immediately, and repeat your remark about hearing from others, smiling as you say it, then turn away and look at others.

Do not get into arguments and always try to keep calm and in control, especially since this type of person may get perverse pleasure from making you lose your cool and look foolish. You might wish to offer to continue the discussion later, but you can always decide to stop it right away and get back to the topic and include others in the discussion.

Again, do not use any put-downs or make facetious remarks, since these will only backfire.

4. Passives

Those who are too active can disrupt your presentation and so can those who are not active enough. The quiet ones are just as damaging to your learning climate, whether their silence is well meant or not. There are two types of quiet people:

(a) The quiet ones (who often sit at the back), who appear withdrawn and do not join in or volunteer comments, or seem willing to answer questions.

(b) Those who give out signals that they really are not interested or do not see the relevance.

People who display these behaviors may have been forced to attend your session or feel they are too important to be there. Sometimes they may spend their time during the session doing other work, such as writing memos or answering their mail! Some, however, might be preoccupied because they are genuinely too busy at this time.

If participants aren't involved in what you're saying, they disrupt anyone else's chances to learn.

Never assume that those who are quiet and do not volunteer or participate actively are actually not really involved and feel negatively about attending. Some individuals are listeners and get a lot out of your session by listening. By observing them well, you will see that they are paying careful attention and participating in their own way. Others may be shy or unassertive or more comfortable on a one-to-one basis. Again, careful observation will show you this.

Remember that you will probably encounter significant cultural differences in participants. It is my experience that, in mixed groups, some women are less likely to express themselves freely. Each participant has his or her own cultural background and it just may not be part of someone's cultural upbringing to speak in a large group.

In chapter 1, we discussed how it was necessary not to base an entire presentation on your own learning style. In the same sense, you also have to consider how your cultural background will influence your presenting style. Let participants know that you want them to feel comfortable. Encourage participation and questions, but don't put people under pressure to speak out. You can encourage them by smiling and rewarding any contributions they might make. After a while, you might ask them a question or ask for a comment on something about which you are aware they are knowledgeable or in which they have particular experience. Make it very low-key and do not put them on the spot. Some passive people do well in small group activities; if possible, ensure that they are not in a group with someone who is too dominant.

It would be nice if participation could be limited just to those who really want to be there! If people are sent to be "improved," they will rarely gain a great deal, and they will possibly prevent others gaining much either, unless they are handled well. You might want to suggest to the client or organizer of the session that they screen out people who really don't want to participate so that you don't end up with hostile people casting a negative atmosphere over your seminar or workshop.

5. Slow learners

Individuals vary in the rate at which they comprehend new information. You will have to exercise some judgment when dealing with the situation where the majority of the group is having no problems, but one individual needs more time than the others or a great deal of your help and attention. You might offer to give that person more time, to see him or her later, or give the rest of the group other work to do, but this is a situation which has no one set answer.

There are times when you genuinely might believe that an individual will never make the grade, no matter how much time and effort is devoted to instructing and learning. This is a problem that my

hairdressing instructors encounter from time to time. Many of them suggest that you do not make too hasty a decision since there are "late developers" around. However, they all say that, sooner or later, you have to discuss reality with such individuals. They are particularly concerned about letting such students go on until the end, only to fail the exam and the course, with the subsequent blow to their self-esteem and pocketbook! Usually they prefer to counsel such students earlier, in the nicest possible way, but still let the student decide whether to continue or not.

b. YOUR OWN PROBLEMS

If you feel at all nervous or anxious, do not let everyone know about this by saying how nervous you are. This only draws attention to your problems and usually makes you even worse than you were before you mentioned it! Most of the time you probably do not appear to be as nervous as you may feel. And, in fact, feeling just a little anxious is probably quite a good thing, because you are less likely to be complacent and are more likely to try to do well.

A key factor in reducing anxiety to a manageable level is being well prepared, having everything you need ready and available, and anticipating potential problems so that you can either prevent them or, at least, have made contingency plans. All of this will build your confidence level and decrease your stress level.

There are ways to make yourself as physically prepared and as comfortable as possible. The following points show how you can deal with various physical problems:

(a) Avoid drinking coffee or other caffeinated drinks since they increase anxiety and aggravate related physical problems (including the need for frequent trips to the washroom!)

(b) If you start to stammer and stutter, slow down, take a deep breath before speaking and do not try to speak until your sentence is completely formed in your mind.

(c) If your legs tremble, do some stretching exercises just before the presentation. During your presentation, flex your legs and alternately tense and relax them.

(d) If your hands start to shake before a presentation, exercise them by squeezing something as hard as you can for five seconds, then relax for about ten seconds. Repeat this until you feel under control.

(e) To handle stomach rumbles, eat regularly. Do not chew gum. Sit up straight or stand up so you do not twist your torso. Talk more loudly if necessary; move further away from the group.

(f) If you are prone to blushing or tend to get too warm, avoid caffeine because it increases your heart rate, blood pressure, and body temperature. Always wear lighter clothing than you think you will need, and in layers, so that you can take off a jacket, if this is appropriate. Perhaps lower the temperature in the room so it is still comfortable but cool enough to maintain attention, too.

(g) For a sudden memory loss (or fears of this happening), take a deep breath and start again. Do not put yourself under pressure by trying to memorize much of what you plan to say. Even if you do remember it all, you could still end up sounding like a parrot, with little or no spontaneity. You will also probably be terrified at the prospect of being asked a question because such an interruption might throw you.

As I have already suggested, have a good set of notes for yourself, to which you can refer when necessary. You will be more comfortable just knowing you have your notes available, even if you do not have to use them a lot.

There is also nothing wrong in admitting that your mind has blanked out for a moment. Most people understand, you can even make a joke of it and come across as more "human." We often create stress for ourselves by trying to be perfect when it is really not necessary.

"I thought I could, I thought I could...": a parting thought

By the time you have worked your way through this book, you will either feel fired up with enthusiasm and ready to go or — and I sincerely hope not — overwhelmed by everything you have to think about before leading a workshop! But take heart. It may well take some time and practice, but, like my friend Peter at the beginning of this, you have already got a lot going for you.

You are obviously interested in your area of expertise and you have your own knowledge.

Start by considering all those positives — the things you have on your side, then use this book to help you develop and continually improve your skills at leading workshops, seminars, and training sessions. Good luck!

Appendix 1
Icebreakers

Here are some suggestions for getting your workshop, seminar, or training session off to a good start.

1. As each participant enters the room at the start of your session or seminar, check off his or her name on your list but give that person *someone else's* name tag. Explain that he or she should look for the person who matches the name tag, introduce himself or herself, and find out a little about the other person.

   (**Note:** You'll want to pair the name tags ahead of time. That is, give Mary John's tag and give John Mary's tag. Otherwise, your "pairs" may never find each other as each is trying to find someone else!)

2. Ask each participant to say what their best job ever was — or who their best boss ever was — and why. If some are uncomfortable saying these out loud, ask them to write it down, hand it in, and then you can read the responses anonymously. Alternatively, you can have participants work in groups and present one group report.

3. Write the names of famous people on cards; one card is then pinned on the back of each person without that person having read the card. Have the group form pairs. Each member of the pair looks at the name on the other person's back; then each takes a turn asking questions in an attempt to guess their own famous name. Questions must be formed so that only yes or no replies can be given. Whoever guesses first, wins.

   For example, you might ask, "Am I a movie star?" "Am I female?" "Am I alive?" etc.

4. Ask participants to stand up and talk about what they would do if they won $1 million in a lottery.

5. Ask each participant to talk for a few minutes on a type of animal he or she would like to be and explain why.

6. Provide small jigsaw puzzles for teams to complete within a certain time limit. This can be especially stimulating if you prearrange for some pieces to be duplicated and some to be missing from each puzzle, forcing teams to trade with each other and work as a larger, negotiating group.

7. Ask the participants to go to the four corners of the room according to these categories: those who are the oldest in their families; those who are the youngest; those who are any place in the middle; those who are only children. As the groups form, ask them to discuss what they liked or disliked about their birth order position. After each group has 10 to 15 minutes to talk, have one person from each group report to the entire group.

8. Ask the participants to describe their names. Each should tell his or her full name, any nickname or abbreviation used, who he or she was named after, and whether he or she likes the name. It's also fun to have each participant say what other name he or she would choose if given the opportunity.

9. Collect several limericks. Write one line of each on individual pieces of paper, but don't write the fifth line on any of them. Give each participant one sheet each and tell them to seek out the other three participants with the lines that fit that particular limerick. Once the group of four is together, they must create the fifth and final line. You could give a small prize to the most creative.

Appendix 2
Resources and suggestions for reading

a. BOOKS

Speak Like a Pro in Business and Public Speaking, Margaret M. Bedrosian

Warmups for Meeting Leaders, Sue Bianchi and Jan Butler

Effective Meetings, Clyde W. Burleson

Use Your Head, Tony Buzan

Make the Most of Your Mind, Tony Buzan

The Winning Trainer - Winning Ways to Involve People in Learning, Julius E. Eitingten

The Winning Image, James Gray

How to Talk So People Listen, Sonya Hamilton

The Business of Public Speaking, Herman Holtz

Preparing Instructional Objectives, Robert F. Mager

Developing Vocational Instruction, Robert F. Mager

The Warmup Manual, Nell Warren Associates

Games Trainers Play: Experiential Learning Exercises, John Newstrom

Teaching and Learning Styles - Celebrating Differences, Ontario Secondary School Teachers' Federation

Body Language: how to read others' thoughts by their gestures, Allan Pease

Presentations Plus, David Peoples

1991 - Annual Developing Human Resources, William Pfeiffer

Making Successful Presentations, Terry C. Smith

Present Yourself With Impact, Caryl Winter

b. AUDIOVISUAL

The Floor Is Yours — Now. Produced by Guild Sound. Leader's guide, booklet: *A Guide to Successful Presentations*. Available in film or video format.

Effective Presentation Skills. Produced by L & K International. Leader's guide and participant workbooks. Available in film or video format.

You'll Soon Get the Hang Of It. Produced by Video Arts, John Cleese's film company. Available in film or video format. Excellent for how to (and how not to!) pass on knowledge and skills in a work setting.

Coaching. Produced by McGraw Hill. Available in film or videocassette format. Again, very good on how to pass on skills at work.

Focus on Adult Learning. Produced by TV Ontario for the TV Ontario Home Studies course. This is a series of television programs which can be augmented with the learning package. For further information phone: 1-800-663-1800, ext. 11; in Toronto phone: 445-5333, ext. 11.

c. PROFESSIONAL ASSOCIATIONS

The American Society for Training and Development; their Training and Developmental Journal

The Ontario Society for Training and Development

OTHER TITLES IN THE
SELF-COUNSEL BUSINESS SERIES

EFFECTIVE SPEAKING FOR BUSINESS SUCCESS
Making presentations, using audio-visuals, and more
by Jacqueline Dunckel and
Elizabeth Parnham

Give dynamic speeches, presentations, and media interviews. When you are called upon to speak in front of your business colleagues, or asked to represent your company in front of the media, do you communicate your thoughts effectively? Or do you become tongue-tied, nervous, and worry about misrepresenting yourself and your business?

Effective communication has always been the key to business success, and this book provides a straightforward approach to developing techniques to improve your on-the-job speaking skills. This book is as easy to pick up and use as a quick reference for a specific problem as it is to read from cover to cover. Whether you want to know how to deal with the media, when to use visual aids in a presentation, or how to prepare for chairing a meeting, this book will answer your questions and help you regain your confidence. $8.95

Contents include:
- Preparing your presentation
- When and where will you speak?
- Let's look at visual aids
- Let's hear what you have to say: rehearsing
- How do you sound?

BUSINESS ETIQUETTE
Make a good impression — gain the competitive edge
by Jacqueline Dunckel

Mind your manners and get ahead! Knowing when to open the door for a colleague or how to accept a gift can sometimes mean the difference between being pigeon-holed in your current position or being offered that attractive promotion. But times have also changed, and the rules once relied on are not always appropriate today. With the growing number of women in company boardrooms and the move toward more international business, a new style of behavior is often called for.

This book is as easy to pick up and use as a quick reference before that special event as it is to read cover to cover. $9.95

Contents include:
- To begin at the beginning — the etiquette of employment
- Department decorum
- Telephone manners
- Meeting manners and boardroom behavior
- Introductions and conversation
- Cultural courtesy
- Table manners
- Eating in and dining out
- Giving and receiving — the etiquette of business gifts
- Manners on the road

A SMALL BUSINESS GUIDE TO EMPLOYEE SELECTION
Finding, interviewing, and hiring the right people
by Lin Grensing

This book offers employers practical information on how to successfully select productive employees. It includes sample advertisements, application forms, suggested interview questions, and role-play exercises for the inter-viewer/applicant exchange. $7.95

Some of the questions answered are:

- What do I need to know before I advertise for the new position?

- How do I screen resumes effectively?

- What questions should I ask the candidates during the interview?

- Do I have to worry about human rights laws when I am hiring?

- What if an employee has AIDS?

- What should I consider before introducing a drug-testing plan at my company?

- What is the best way to make a new employee feel comfortable? How can top employees be encouraged to stay?

MOTIVATING TODAY'S WORK FORCE
When the carrot can't always be cash
Lin Grensing

In the 1990s, a favorable working environment combined with good worker benefits will eclipse salaries as the prime concern of the work force. Here is a book that tackles the job-satisfaction issue head on. It offers creative options that will help companies increase worker effectiveness. The book shows owners and managers what their employees value most, whether it's a simple pat on the back or an innovative non-monetary reward such as an in-house day-care center or more independence.

Lin Grensing knows the best-kept secrets on how to boost the bottom line by improving productivity through honest praise, promotions, and perks. Her book gives practical applications to various motivational theories and shows how to attain a high level of corporate morale in that all-important work force. $8.95

Contents include:

- Nonmonetary incentives and motivational theory

- How to avoid the motivational fallacies

- How to determine what motivates employees

- Goal setting

- Communication

- Job enrichment

- Flexible benefits

PRODUCING A FIRST-CLASS VIDEO FOR YOUR BUSINESS
Work with professionals or do it yourself
by Dell Dennison, Don Doman, and Margaret Doman

Whether you want to sell and demonstrate your product, build your corporate image, announce new items to the media, train employees, or educate the public about your cause, presenting your message on video may be the answer for you. This book tells you everything you need to know about finding and working with a video production company, or doing it yourself and setting up your own production facility. It offers tips on everything from preparing your employees to appear on camera to making your office look good on video. $14.95

Topics covered include:

- Determining if video is the best way to reach your audience
- Planning your budget and estimating costs
- Finding the right production company
- Writing the script
- Using music, special effects,graphics, and interactive video
- Hiring professional performers or using employees
- Shooting on location or in the studio
- Editing and the postproduction process

KEEPING CUSTOMERS HAPPY
Strategies for success
by Jacqueline Dunckel and Brian Taylor

Customer satisfaction is your company's best asset!

Consumers today demand personal attention from businesses before they spend their money. So, customer service is moving up the priority list in dynamic companies and it is consuming more of their time and budgets; businesses that ignore customer relations do so at their peril.

You need good service to attract customers and keep them coming back, and this book provides plans and programs that have been proven successful by other businesses. No matter what kind of business you are in, this book will help increase profits through improved customer relations. $8.95

Contents include:

- Customer service — what it is and what it is not
- The "why" of customer relations
- The value of service
- Developing a profitable customer relations program
- Setting goals for your business
- Putting your plan together
- Communicating your customer relations program to your employees
- Training employees
- Bringing it all together

PRACTICAL TIME MANAGEMENT
How to get more things done in less time
by Bradley C. McRae

Here is sound advice for anyone who needs to develop practical time management skills. It is designed to help any busy person, from any walk of life, use his or her time more effectively. Not only does it explain how to easily get more things done, it shows you how your self-esteem will improve in doing so. More important, emphasis is placed on maintenance so that you remain in control. Whether you want to find extra time to spend with your family or read the latest bestseller, this book will give you the guidance you need — without taking up a lot of your time! $7.95

Some of the skills you will learn are:

- Learning to monitor where your time goes
- Setting realistic and attainable goals
- Overcoming inertia
- Rewarding yourself
- Planning time with others
- Managing leisure time
- Planning time for hobbies and vacations
- Maintaining the new you

ORDER FORM

All prices are subject to change without notice. Books are available in book, department, and stationery stores. If you cannot buy the book through a store, please use this order form. (Please print)

Name _____

Address _____

_____

Charge to: ❑Visa   ❑ MasterCard

Account Number _____

Validation Date _____

Expiry Date_____

Signature_____

❑Check here for a free catalogue.

IN CANADA
Please send your order to the nearest location:
Self-Counsel Press
1481 Charlotte Road
North Vancouver, B. C.
V7J 1H1

Self-Counsel Press
8-2283 Argentia Road
Mississauga, Ontario
L5N 5Z2

IN THE U.S.A.
Please send your order to:
Self-Counsel Press Inc.
1704 N. State Street
Bellingham, WA 98225

YES, please send me:

_____copies of **Effective Speaking for Business Success**, $8.95

_____copies of **Business Etiquette**, $9.95

_____copies of **A Small Business Guide to Employee Selection**, $7.95

_____copies of **Motivating Today's Work Force**, $8.95

_____copies of **Producing a First-Class Video For Your Business**, $14.95

_____copies of **Keeping Customers Happy**, $8.95

_____copies of **Practical Time Management**, $7.95

Please add $2.50 for postage & handling. Canadian residents, please add 7% GST to your order.
WA residents, please add 7.8% sales tax.